CHRISTOPHER STOAKES

IS LAW FOR YOU?

DECIDING IF YOU WANT TO STUDY LAW

ΧΦΣ

British library cataloguing-in-publication data

A catalogue record for this book is available from the British Library.

Published by:
Christopher Stoakes Ltd
Marlowe House
Hale Road
Wendover
Bucks
HP22 6NE

ISBN: 978-0-9574946-2-6

Second edition published March 2013.

Printed and bound in Great Britain.

Written by Christopher Stoakes; researched and edited by Viola Joseph.

Written, researched and edited at Scripto KT, Studio WO, Mews WO and Astoria DM.

© Christopher Stoakes 2013

The CSL logo incorporating the Greek device is a registered trademark.

What This Book Is About

You are thinking of studying law or becoming a lawyer. But what is law really like? How does it feel, being a lawyer, and what do lawyers do all day?

Be warned. The law may not be what you expect.

If you think it's a well-ordered city with wide, straight boulevards, beautiful public buildings and graceful office blocks that have developed over the centuries, you are in for a shock.

It's more like a shanty town with shifting streets, darkened alleyways, dead-ends, cul-de-sacs, lanes that shoot off in opposite directions and some thoroughfares that can disappear almost overnight. In short it can appear a bewildering maze. What you need is a map.

This book provides that map. It offers a unique insight into the law and its practice. It covers the key topics in a new and engrossing way that will help you decide whether the law really is for you.

Who This Book Is For

- Anyone who is thinking of studying law and wants to find out what law is like.
- Anyone who is thinking of becoming a lawyer.
- Anyone who is intrigued by law and wants to know what it is really like and why.
- Anyone who might be affected by the law at some point in their lives and wants to be prepared.

Who This Book Is By

Chris Stoakes knows more about lawyers and law than most people.

He has been a City solicitor, a partner in a law firm, a legal journalist and editor, a law teacher, a tutor on an MBA for lawyers and a management consultant advising law firms and in-house legal departments. He is an award-winning designer of innovative legal training programmes and has trained lawyers in effective writing and commercial awareness.

Chris has held various senior positions in law firms, including head of legal training and director of marketing. Most recently, he has been director of knowledge management at a top ten global law firm.

Chris read law at Worcester College, Oxford and qualified at Freshfields.

Note On This 2nd Edition

This is the second edition of *Is Law For You?*

The first edition was published in 2011. The difference between the two is that the first edition was autobiographical. Each chapter on the law was prefaced by an anecdote from Chris Stoakes's legal career and the book's sub-title was: *One Man's Life In And Around Law*.

This edition removes those references to make it a shorter, quicker and more direct read. Some minor cases have been omitted but the discussion of the law remains the same.

CONTENTS

LEGAL PERIODIC TABLE

LAW IN THEORY		
WHAT THE LAW IS	***The five pillars of law*** Criminal Tort Contract Property Equity	
	Common law in context Common law v civil law Comparative law English law v New York law Private international law Public international law	
	Philosophy of law Jurisprudence	
LAW IN PRACTICE		
HOW LAW DEVELOPS (See Appendix for full list)	***Types of law*** Banking Commercial Company Competition Construction Employment Environmental	Insurance Intellectual property Matrimonial Media Pensions Shipping Tax Welfare
HOW LAW IS MADE	***Parliament*** Administrative & constitutional law English legal history Law reform	
HOW LAW IS APPLIED	***The courts*** English legal system Criminal v civil Judges	Damages Legal aid Contingency fees Prison (recidivism)
WHAT LAWYERS DO	***The legal profession*** Barrister v solicitor Contentious v non-contentious High street v City Legal aid v private client In-house v private practice Corporate v public sector National v international	

This table is explained at the end of Summing Up.

INTRODUCTION

If you tell your parents (as I did) that you want to become a lawyer (as I did) then a big, shark-like grin will break out all over their faces.

Because every mum and dad wants his or her son or daughter to be a lawyer (without necessarily having to be one themselves).

You can earn tons of dosh, your mates will respect you and no one, in this modern and complex society that is underpinned by law, will be able to leg you over.

It will give your parents loads of bragging rights over neighbours, distant relatives, etc, etc ('Yes, well, actually, Little Johnny is at the Bar') and all of that false modesty rubbish (although if your parents put it like that the less informed may think you've developed an alcohol-abuse issue).

So this book is for you.

Because once you've told your mum and dad, you can't not deliver, can you?

What's It All About?

But what is it like, exactly, this law thing? And what is it like being a lawyer? And is there just one type of lawyer or many? And what do they do all day to earn these piles of gold? And how much gold is it exactly? And how much of your soul do you have to sell to the devil to get it all?

Because one of the bizarre things about the law is that most students who study it at uni do so without having tried it before. Law at A level is not a popular option. This means you can sign up for as much as three years of undergraduate law at uni without knowing if you're going to like it.

There are alternatives, of course. You can do something else you really love for your degree and then do what is (currently) called the GDL (Graduate Diploma in Law) – a one-year conversion course. Sounds good. Problem: the fees alone will set you back £10,000; and you need to have done a degree.

On top of that it's a hell of an immersion: a year to absorb what undergrads do in two or three. But even after that you've still got to do the LPC (Legal Practice Course) to be a solicitor or the BPTC (Bar Professional Training Course) to be a barrister – and how do you know which you want to be if you've never tried either before?

Of course you can dispense with the degree route completely. Instead you can do the CILEx course (CILEx = Chartered Institute of Legal Executives). This is delivered mainly by further education (FE) colleges for people in work or maternity returners and is a five-year programme of evening and weekend study. It's an excellent course.

Problem: it doesn't make you a solicitor (although there is a further conversion route to follow). And if you're working during the day it's hard to study at night: the only student I've ever had fall asleep on me in class was working in a solicitor's by day, flipping hamburgers at Gatwick by night and fitting in my CILEx evening classes in between.

So this book is a way in. A way in to help you decide whether you might want to do the law for real. And if that's too late – if that's all behind you and you regret never having given it a go or having had the chance, then this book is a way of experiencing what you missed. I don't think it's ever too late.

And what if you're none of these things? What if you've never had the chance to be a lawyer but you feel you want to know about it, this law thing, so you don't end up being done to or over by the law? Or what if you already have been done over and feel you're a victim of law? What then? Well, this book will tell you enough to be able to get into the subject of law yourself so you need never feel intimidated by it or by these glossy, silver-tongued legal eagles ever again.

You see, despite its reputation for being difficult and dull (what a combination!) the law is actually interesting and important. It affects us all. Which is a good reason why we should all know a bit about it.

Who This Book Is For

So this book is for anyone who's interested in the law but isn't a lawyer – especially for anyone who's thinking of becoming one. This book is for:

- Anyone who is thinking of studying law and wants to find out what law is like.
- Anyone who is thinking of becoming a lawyer.
- Anyone who is intrigued by law and wants to know what it is really like and why.
- Anyone who might be affected by the law at some point in their lives and wants to be prepared.

Basically, all of us.

Learning The Law

And what do you find, when you sign up to study law? What do you find when you open the first law book (and there are certainly loads of law books to study)?

Well I'll tell you what I found: a complete and utter shambles.

Let me explain. As a kid at school I never got chemistry as a subject. Even the Periodic Table in those days was a total nightmare. It had bits hanging off the ends and some bits that seemed not to be that much connected at all. Scientists still seemed to be able to find new elements and add them to it. It made no sense to me, so neither did chemistry. Who knew what you would get if you stuck some carbon sulphate crystals in a solution? Why would you even bother?

Well, just imagine my shock when I started studying law.

I had thought the law would be nice and ordered, a set of rules written down in a book (well, several books – as I say, I knew there was likely to be a lot of it because people always said it was a demanding subject).

I thought it would be like a vast marble temple, built to a grand Palladian design, symmetrical, ordered, unchanging, universal.

But it wasn't anything like that at all. It was more like a shanty town, a jumble. It consisted of principles and exceptions to those principles, and exceptions to the exceptions to those principles, and exceptions to the exceptions to the exceptions to the principles. There were bits still under construction and other bits that had been started and abandoned. Other bits had been built, torn down and fenced off. There were blind alleys and dead ends and subjects that overlapped or – worse still – had nothing to do with each other at all. Bits had been added on here and lopped off there. Extensions had been started then stopped. New areas opened up but no one quite knew where they were heading or when they'd be finished. Some bits were always changing. Other bits never changed. Some bits even the people who inhabited them couldn't work out at all or, at least, they seemed to be in constant argument with each other over.

Then there was a parallel universe. There was a whole area called law and then another area called equity that judges invented to get round the law. What's more judges often contradicted each other. Courts reversed each other. Parliament passed laws that looked as if they were written in English but which you couldn't even read out loud let alone grasp, and which were hundreds of pages long.

Then there was the Latin – don't get me started on the Latin: caveat emptor; res ipsa loquitur; volenti non fit injuria; contra proferentem. And there were weird expressions like 'the man on the Clapham omnibus'; the 'reasonable bystander'; 'the bona fide purchaser for value without notice'.

Even going to court – which seemed to me a basic part of law – seemed difficult. There were different courts to choose from (one called the Queen's Bench and another called Chancery) and there was a whole raft of evidence you couldn't use because of something called the 'hearsay rule' and then – beat this – you had to tell your opponent your evidence before you could use it! How stupid is that! Sometimes when you wrote to the other side you could say the letter was 'without prejudice' which seemed to make it invisible as if you hadn't written it at all.

Even in something as basic as land law (what could be simpler than the stuff you stand on?) there were things called 'easements' and 'overriding interests' and 'restrictive covenants' (the 'negative' ones were said to 'run with the land' and the 'positive' ones didn't – as if we were suddenly dealing with electricity) and the worst sin of all was to buy something called a 'flying freehold' (does land fly?). The whole thing was frankly bizarre.

And there was a whole area of law that does your head in about what justice is and whether law is good and what it's got to do with society, a kind of philosophy of law called 'jurisprudence'. The arguments over in that part of town were even worse with loads of people standing round in distinct groups barely speaking to each other.

Eggshell Skull

Whole new areas of law would be created just because someone found a slug in a ginger beer bottle. Did you know you could be guilty of murder because someone had an eggshell skull (what is an eggshell skull; would it make a good name for a rock band)? Or that a key part of contract law revolved around a shopkeeper displaying a penknife in the window? Or that a famous judge (now dead) called Lord Denning created legal history with a judgment that started: 'It was bluebell time in Kent'?

And areas could disappear too. For a long time when I was a student there was a black hole in contract law called 'fundamental breach', which you skirted round with especial care. When I came back to write this book three decades later it had completely disappeared, concreted over, just like that. Weird, huh?

In fact one of the greatest descriptions of English common law (don't worry, all these weird and wonderful terms will be explained) is that of a tree root which inches its way forward in the darkness, feeling its way round the stones and obstacles it encounters. When, much later, the stones and obstacles have disappeared as well as the root itself, the twisted channel of that root is still there, forever imprinted in the ground, a bit like ox-bow lakes when rivers dry up. Same with the law. You can trace where it is now in its past patterns. And they go all over the place. (Yes, that's a subject in its own right too, called 'English Legal History'.)

Well, you can imagine my bafflement. Possibly even worse than that was the feeling that I was on my own. People around me who were also studying law seemed to get it immediately. They could speak the language and find their way around no trouble, virtually overnight, while I had to toil away trying to squeeze a small amount of understanding out of a big pile of work. At times I felt like crying (at times I did).

I vowed then that if I had anything to do with the law it would be to open it up for the rest of us. As it happens I did become a lawyer, in a prestigious City law firm. But there were other things I wanted to do, too. I became a journalist, an editor and a teacher. I became a marketing director and a management consultant (and even a partner in a law firm). Despite all these different roles, I've spent most of my working life in and around lawyers and law firms – in fact I couldn't have done any of it without being a lawyer. I've found that the best lawyers are strange but brilliant people whom I have to say I love even though some of them couldn't find their way round Sainsbury's and find life outside the law completely bewildering – but we'll get on to that later. And in my last and final job in the law I've been responsible for the training of lawyers and curating their legal know-how at one of the largest law firms in the world.

And now, finally, I think I kind of 'get' it. Which is why I have written this book. So you can get it too.

Getting Started

Almost all law books start off with ELS ('English Legal System'): how law is made and decided; what Parliament does and how the law courts work. Sounds sensible, doesn't it? But in fact it's the kiss of death. It's so BORING.

Don't start there. Start with the guy with the eggshell skull or the shopkeeper with the knife in the window. Start with the slug in the bottle. But don't start with ELS. Talking of slugs in bottles, I have to tell you a funny but true story: years after the slug case a food manufacturer accidentally left a caterpillar in a tin of peas. The consumer sued. So the manufacturer counterclaimed – and took the case all the way to the House of Lords (then the top court in the land) – on the basis that the consumer had got more protein than they had paid for. Good, eh? Don't you just love lawyers!

So, I am not starting with ELS. No, I'm going to start with something much more interesting.

I'm going to start with murder. And what I want to know is this: would you defend a murderer?

CHAPTER 1

CRIME

Defendant – accused – verdict – convicted – defence – prosecution – murder – act – intention – actus reus – mens rea – manslaughter – reckless – held – overruled – subjective test – grievous bodily harm (GBH) – specific intent – basic intent – rex – regina – head – voluntary manslaughter – involuntary manslaughter – causation – novus actus interveniens – eggshell skull – year and a day – omissions – special relationship – penal code – crimes against the person – assault – battery – apprehending – sex crimes – stalking – offences against property – theft – robbery – burglary – criminal damage – handling stolen goods – fraud – attempt – conspire – incite – inchoate – accomplice – assisted suicide – administrative offences – driving offences – defences – plea in mitigation – distinguish – hard cases

Well, would you defend a murderer?

I know. I can tell you're already there: it's a trick question, isn't it?

The right answer is: who says he is (by the way I'm going to call him D for **defendant** and by saying 'him' I mean 'her' too)?

Who says D is a murderer?

D is only a murderer once the court has said he is. That's the whole point of the trial. He is **accused** of murder, but only after the trial has ended and a **verdict** has been given ('handed down' as they say in the States which has caught on here in the UK too) and he has been **convicted**, is he actually a murderer.

But supposing he is caught red-handed (so to speak: the knife in his hand and his hand covered in blood). What then? It's obvious, isn't it that he – or she – did it?

Well, the question then is: did what? The victim (whom I'll call V) may be dead. But it may have been an accident. Or V might have attacked D and D was only defending himself. Or V may have provoked D. Or D may suffer from a medical condition which meant he didn't know what he was doing. Are all of those murder too?

Evidently not: it's a matter of circumstance, motive and degree (and, indeed, of evidence).

It's at this point that we actually have to define what murder is to know what we're talking about. So let's do that.

But, before I tell you what the legal definition of murder is, let's pause there. Are you enjoying this? Do you see this as splitting hairs or as really interesting? If the former, chuck this book away or give it to someone else who you think may like it more than you. Whatever. But if this hasn't grabbed you, I think you may find law dull and difficult.

Maybe you're not sure yet. Maybe the, er, jury is still out (we do juries later on). Anyway, let's plough on.

So, where we've got to is that the whole point of defending someone accused of being a murderer is that you don't know whether they are one or not. That's for the court to decide. Until a court has decided that someone is guilty of murder, they aren't (this is the fundamental principle of English criminal law that you are innocent until proved guilty). And it's for the **defence** lawyer to argue that they aren't and the **prosecution** lawyer to show why they are. It's this collision of arguments over which the court presides that forges the right outcome, that creates justice (we'll come back later to who these lawyers are and which court they're in – for the moment it's not important).

So, in short, whether or not D is guilty of murder depends on how you define the crime of murder. So close your eyes and imagine how, if you were the Supreme Legislator of the Known Universe, you would define murder.

Then write it down.

Once you've had a go at that, read on.

OK, done that? Here we go. Compare yours to this.

Murder

At its most basic **murder** is *killing* someone because you *mean* to (there's a lot more to it than that, but I want to start simple if you don't mind):

- Killing someone means: doing something as a result of which they die.
- Meaning to means: having the intention to do so.

So already we've teased out the two principal components of a crime (in this case the crime of murder): an **act** and an **intention**.

D needs to do something (act); with the intention of doing it (intent).

The act is called the **actus reus**. Actus is the Latin word from which we get 'action' and of course 'act' itself. Reus comes from res meaning 'thing'. So actus reus means 'action thing'. 'Thing' doesn't quite do res justice, given that we get words like reality, realisation and republic (res publica = 'public thing') from it.

The intent is called the **mens rea**. Mens means 'mind' (hence 'mental'). So mens rea means 'mental thing'.

So the crime of murder needs actus reus and mens rea. We're going to look at mens rea first, then come back to actus reus.

Mens Rea = Intent

So mens rea is intending to kill V. But what about this, though: what if D didn't mean to kill V?

What if D didn't intend to kill V but V died anyway? Suppose D only meant to hit V but V died from the blow? Then the law says D is not guilty of murder but is guilty of a lesser crime (since V did die, after all). This crime is **manslaughter**. Manslaughter is still extremely serious: D will still be guilty of a serious crime but the punishment won't be as bad as for murder.

Mens Rea Falling Short Of Intent To Kill

But suppose D didn't mean to kill V but at the same time didn't care what happened to V? In law this is called recklessness or being **reckless**. It means doing something without having any regard for the consequences. Nowadays that

3

would still be manslaughter on the basis that D lacked the requisite intent required for murder. But it wasn't always so.

In the past it did amount to murder: not giving a damn. For a long time, if D was reckless about whether he or she did kill V, then that was the same as actually meaning to, and so therefore was murder.

This followed from a case called *Caldwell* (1981) in which D was convicted of arson. D was drunk at the time and didn't know what he was doing. He lit the fire to keep warm but without any thought (because he was so drunk) as to the consequences, which in legal terms is being reckless. Nobody was killed. But arson (burning a building down) is regarded in law as pretty serious and the intent for arson is the same as for murder. So whatever the court held sufficient for intent here would apply equally to murder.

The top court (at the time the House of Lords) **held** (the legal term for 'decided') that D had intent even if he hadn't considered the risk involved because, looked at objectively, what he did (lighting a fire in a derelict warehouse) was reckless, and that was enough. Now, although this case had nothing to do with murder, it had everything to do with intent: the same test applied in murder as in arson. For a while it seemed that murder didn't require D to intend death; only that he was reckless as to whether death might result from his actions.

But *Caldwell* was followed by a string of cases involving kids messing around with matches and petrol and burning places down without really grasping fully the risks of what they were doing. It was harsh to convict them in the absence of that intent. So, about 20 years later, the House of Lords in another criminal case **overruled** *Caldwell* and substituted a **subjective test** of whether D was actually himself aware of the risk. If he wasn't, then he lacked intent sufficient for murder or arson. He didn't have the requisite mens rea.

However, where D intends **grievous bodily harm** (known colloquially as **GBH** and considered to be almost as serious as murder) and V dies as a result, D can be guilty of murder and not 'just' GBH, because it represents sufficient disregard for human life. Again, what D actually intended is key. He needs at least to have intended GBH to be guilty of murder if V dies. So intention is subjective: it's what D himself actually intended in relation to V. The fact that death or GBH is the natural consequence of D's actions isn't enough to remove the need for intent.

The Law Commission (a body which makes recommendations for improvements in the law) has suggested a crime of 'second degree murder' where reckless indifference would be sufficient mens rea. This is essentially 'not caring a damn' about the consequences and used to be the test for the old definition of rape (reckless indifference as to whether V consented). This is different from reckless stupidity of the type that occurred in *Caldwell*.

So you can perhaps begin to see that the law draws a distinction between crimes of **specific intent** (required, for instance, for murder, where the motive is specific to a particular V) and crimes of **basic intent** (that is, crimes capable of being committed recklessly without any particular V in mind). Crimes of specific intent cannot be committed recklessly. They include murder and theft. Crimes of basic intent include manslaughter, assault, battery and rape (all of which we'll come to later).

OK, let's pause here. Are you enjoying this? I'm not asking you to even begin to understand it (having just re-read the last few paragraphs I'm not sure I do). So this isn't about whether you understand the objective test of recklessness. I'm simply asking whether you like the thought process required to think this through and whether you mind that law changes over time. Law is like riding a bike: some people get it first time; others (like me) keep falling off and getting back on until one miraculous day it all seems to fall into place and we wobble off with the handlebars swinging this way and that – but at least we're on our way. Maybe you're like me.

Anyway, while we're having a breather, just an aside on case names. All cases are between two or more parties. But criminal cases are brought by the prosecution, which is the state and is usually written as R for **rex** (Latin for king) or **regina** (Latin for queen) depending on who is the monarch. (We'll see when we look at courts that Queen's Bench and King's Bench are the same court in different reigns.) So a typical criminal case is called *R v Stoakes*, where Stoakes is D and 'v' is short for 'versus'. It is actually spoken as 'and' or 'against' not 'vee'. So *R v Stoakes* would be read out loud as 'R and Stoakes' or 'R against Stoakes'. See: you're beginning to sound like a lawyer already. Sometimes the 'R' is left out: sometimes it's the DPP (Director of Public Prosecutions) or another enforcement agency or even the name of a chief constable.

Manslaughter

So, if that's murder, manslaughter is causing death but without the requisite intent: the actus reus without the requisite mens rea. Manslaughter falls under two heads (**head** rather than heading in law): voluntary and involuntary manslaughter.

Voluntary manslaughter occurs where there is sufficient actus reus and mens rea for murder but D can rely on one of three defences: provocation, diminished responsibility or killing as part of a suicide pact. These reduce a conviction of murder to one of manslaughter. Note that these are examples of wider circumstances called defences that can affect intent. We look at them later.

Involuntary manslaughter applies where the mens rea for murder is absent. There are two types of involuntary manslaughter: unlawful act manslaughter (an unlawful act which is dangerous and causes death); and manslaughter by gross negligence (which overlaps with recklessness).

Adamako (1994) is a case on gross negligence in which an anaesthetist in an operation failed to see that the patient's breathing tube was disconnected for several minutes – a bit like a pilot failing to see a mountain up ahead. The patient died and the anaesthetist was held guilty of manslaughter for gross negligence – not in the sense of considering then completely disregarding a risk (or simply being wilfully blind to it) but just in being plain stupid, but really badly so. Straight negligence is not as serious (doing something without taking proper care) but is at the heart of many more 'administrative' crimes such as 'driving without due care and attention'.

This area of law has thrown up other notable and harrowing cases over the last few decades: *DPP v Newbury* (1977), where a couple of 15 year-olds threw a paving stone off a railway bridge as a train was going past, killing the guard; *Hancock and Shankland* (1986) – in the latter case they were both Ds so the 'and' there really does mean 'and' – when a concrete block was thrown off a bridge during the miners' strike and killed the driver of a taxi on the road below who was ferrying strike-breaking miners to work; and *Woollin* (1998) when a parent lost their temper and killed their child.

Over that period, manslaughter extended into the business world (where it is called corporate manslaughter). Organisations can now be guilty of unlawful killing: for instance through industrial accidents that involve employees (such as maintenance workers knocked down on a railway track) or disasters affecting the public at large (such as a ferry sinking). Cases are brought under the Corporate Manslaughter and Corporate Homicide Act 2007.

Criminal Act = Actus Reus

So far we've been looking at the necessary mens rea for murder and manslaughter. But there can be complications on the actus reus side too. You might think this odd. If someone knifes someone else, the actus reus is pretty obvious isn't it?

Well, maybe.

But suppose D hit V but that isn't what killed V. What killed V was the fact that he fell over from being hit but it was in falling that he banged his head on the pavement and it's that striking of his head on the pavement which killed him.

What then? Can D be said to have caused V's death?

This is a question of **causation**. Did D's act cause V's death? This is also known as the 'but for' test? But for D's act, would V have died? The actus reus doesn't have to be the only cause of death but it has to be a significant factor. An intervening act which removes liability is called a **novus actus interveniens** (yup, Latin again, meaning 'new act intervening').

In *Thabo Meli* (1954) a gang tried to kill V by hitting him over the head. They then chucked his body over a cliff. He was still alive at that point but died from the fall and from exposure at the bottom of the cliff. The Ds argued that these were new intervening acts. The court disagreed and convicted them of murder. By contrast, in *Church* (1966), D mistakenly thought he had killed V so dumped V's body in a canal where V drowned. D was convicted of manslaughter, not murder.

What if V died only because he or she had a thinner skull than normal? This is the **eggshell skull** principle I referred to in the Introduction. It says simply that D must take V as he finds him. So if D hits V and V falls over and dies because V has a thin skull (in circumstances where a person with an ordinary skull would have survived) that does not excuse D. You take your victim as you find them. It is still your fault.

A Year And A Day

An old approach to causation was the year-and-a-day rule. If V died more than a **year and a day** later, D would get off. Presumably this was a reflection of past times when healthcare wasn't that good, so if you survived for a year and then died it could easily be down to something else (a novus actus interveniens, I guess) such as typhoid, tuberculosis or malnutrition, rather than a stab wound from a year before. Medical science is a lot better now so this rule was repealed by the snappily-but-accurately-entitled Murder (Abolition of the Year and a Day Rule) Act 1996.

Omissions

So far D's actus reus has consisted of doing something. **Omissions** (not doing something) rarely attract liability: a bystander who fails to rescue someone may be morally culpable but won't be guilty of a crime.

However, on occasion liability does arise from simply not doing anything at all. So, if a parent neglects their child (for instance through failing to feed the child) and the child dies, that can be manslaughter and even murder. The same applies where D takes on responsibility for someone (such as an elderly relative) and fails to look after them or fails to seek medical help when they suffer illness or injury. Failure to call medical services when the elderly relative is ill which leads to their death can be manslaughter.

In these cases the courts have said there is a **special relationship** between D and V which can expose D to criminal liability. Incidentally, both of those examples (child and vulnerable adult) are now statutory crimes under the Domestic Violence, Crime and Victims Act 2004.

Liability for not doing something also arose in *Fagan v Metropolitan Police Commissioner* (1969) in which D drove on to a policeman's foot by accident then refused to move his car when he realised what he had done. D was hardly going to get away with that. The court found that failing to do so – an omission – was sufficient actus reus.

Right. So far I've been trying to give you a flavour of what criminal law defines as murder and what it says is the lesser crime of manslaughter. But this isn't meant to be a comprehensive review. Just enough (I hope) to whet your appetite. So let's move on. I think we've done murder and manslaughter to death, don't you?

Penal Code. Not

So far we've looked at murder and manslaughter because they are the most serious crimes in that they involve people losing their lives. But there are many other crimes which, taken together, form a kind of criminal menu or catalogue. In some countries this single source of criminal law is published as a **penal code**.

We don't have that in the UK, in the same way that traditionally we never had a written constitution – a reflection of the piecemeal way in which English law develops (for more on this see Chapter 10). But, periodically, different parts of the criminal legal system get overhauled, usually involving the Law Commission (most recently when looking at sex crimes and fraud).

If you haven't already scanned the paragraphs below, repeat the previous game: close your eyes and try to think up the other likely types of crime there might be in addition to those involving unlawful killing.

Done that? OK, my own periodic table of crimes has four categories. I'm not going to cover each of these in turn – after all, this isn't a legal textbook. But I will focus on things I find interesting which I hope you will too. Remember that for all of these, just as for murder and manslaughter, there need to be both actus reus and mens rea.

First, Crimes Against The Person

Crimes against the person include:

- Murder and manslaughter (already covered above)
- Other common offences against the person
    - Grievous bodily harm (known as GBH), assault, battery
    - Sex offences
    - Causing death by dangerous driving
- Other less common offences against people (kidnap, stalking, racially aggravated offences, assisted suicide)

Aside from GBH (mentioned above) the offence against the person that readily springs to mind in the popular imagination is **assault** and **battery** (which is actually two offences, one of assault and the other of battery). Assault is what you and I think of as hitting someone. But actually that's wrong. Battery is hitting someone. Assault is making them think they are about to be hit (**apprehending** that a battery is about to happen).

In fact, assault does not require the victim to be touched at all while battery, for its part, can be committed by the slightest contact (provided V can feel it). Battery can also be indirect (such as using a car to run someone down; or causing a mother to drop a baby she is holding, which is battery on the baby). The mens rea for both is intent or recklessness (not caring what happens).

The other extensive area of non-fatal crimes against the person are **sex crimes** which have been comprehensively codified in the Sexual Offences Act 2003. The area of sex offences used to be particularly complicated. It's hard to believe that homosexual acts were actually against the law until 1967 or that a man could not be guilty of raping a woman if she was his wife. Now the latter has been changed (by the House of Lords in *R v R* (1992)), after a string of cases where courts had – sometimes very reluctantly – said that husbands had their wives' unending consent to sex (even if the wife had filed for divorce in the meantime).

The law has gradually extended to provide protection to cover new circumstances. So, in *Dica* (2003) a man was convicted of grievous bodily harm for knowingly infecting two women with HIV. Which just shows that the law recognises sexual crimes as crimes of violence.

Stalking, for example, is, in a sense, a crime of threatened violence (or, at least, that's how it may feel to V) and has been criminalised by the Stalking (Protection from Harassment) Act 1997. And grooming, made possible by the internet, is now a crime preliminary to, or an aspect of, paedophilia.

Amongst the more recent additions are child kidnap (the Child Abduction Act 1984) and terrorism (many pieces of legislation in recent years, including the Terrorism Acts 2000 and 2006 and the Counter-Terrorism Act 2008).

Talk of kidnap brings me on to the famous legal remedy of *habeas corpus* ('you have the body') but it doesn't have as much to do with crime as you might think. It's actually what's called an administrative remedy (a claim brought against the state by the citizen to make the state do or not do something) and is a way of getting someone released who is being held without charge. We cover administrative remedies later.

Second, Offences Against Property

Offences against property ('crime' and 'offence' mean the same thing) include:

- Theft
- Robbery
- Burglary
- Making off without payment
- Handling stolen goods
- Fraud

As recently as Victorian times, crimes against property were almost more serious than crimes against people, because property was owned by the rich and unlawful killing was more likely to occur at the lowest levels of society where life was short and cheap.

Nowadays, you'll be glad to hear, people come before things (except in Dilbert where they come after tracing paper).

Theft

Any student of modern criminal law begins with the Theft Act 1968 (known as 'TA68' in textbooks). Section 1(1) says that a person is guilty of **theft** if he 'dishonestly appropriates property belonging to another' with the intention of 'permanently depriving' the other of it, which as legal definitions go is brief and to the point.

So, to put this in an everyday context, switching labels in a supermarket to get the higher-priced item at the lower price is an offence – see *Morris* (1984) – which you can be convicted of even if you haven't got to the checkout (*Anderson v Burnside*, also 1984 – maybe a lot of it was going on that year).

Information was not previously regarded as property within the definition of TA68. But it is now covered by the Computer Misuses Act 1990 (which basically outlawed hacking and using viruses). Electricity was another good or service that fell outside the accepted definition of property at the time TA68 was enacted so theft of electricity (for instance by circumventing the metered supply) was covered separately by section 13 TA68. Blackmail is covered by s21 TA68. **Robbery** is theft with force or the threat or fear of force (s8 TA68). The force or threat must be used to steal. Force or threat against the property itself isn't enough. **Burglary** is theft by breaking into someone's home or premises.

In case you're wondering, a different offence against property itself is that of **criminal damage** which can carry a penalty almost as great as that for manslaughter, another throwback to the Victorian idea of the sanctity of property. Crimes against animals also carry a stiff prison sentence (see Animal Welfare Act 2006) which again may be surprising but is a reflection of their comparative defencelessness against inhumane treatment.

If D can't be charged with theft itself, he may still be nicked for **handling stolen goods**. Under s22 TA68 handling stolen goods includes doing, or arranging to do, or assisting with the doing of, any of: receiving (taking stolen goods into possession or control), removing (moving them), realising (selling or exchanging them), disposing (hiding or destroying them) and retaining (keeping them). And 'goods' are defined in s34 to include money and everything else except land (but including things that were attached to the land but were separated from it by stealing). Which is about as comprehensive as you can get.

Fraud

Another area of criminal law which, like sex offences, has been overhauled recently is **fraud**. Before the Fraud Act 2006 there were various offences, spread across at least two separate Theft Acts that were technical in the extreme and ranged from 'obtaining property by deception' (property here meaning almost anything owned by someone else) and 'obtaining a pecuniary advantage by deception', through to obtaining services by deception, obtaining a money transfer and evasion of liability (also by deception).

Two cases will give you an idea of what a minefield this was. In *R v Collis-Smith* (1971) D filled up with petrol then told the garage his employer would pay and drove off. Of course it was a lie. He was prosecuted for obtaining property by deception. But D got off. The court said the deception was not 'operative' since it wasn't made till after the property in the petrol had passed. So D should have been charged with evasion of liability by deception under a different part of the TA68. That one went to the Court of Appeal.

Preddy (1996) went all the way to the House of Lords. Again, D got off. This case involved mortgage fraud but the acts in question (transfers of money between bank accounts) were not deemed to amount to 'obtaining property belonging to another by deception' within s15 of the TA68 (because the money doesn't actually pass from one bank account to another – technically, rights in one account are extinguished and new rights in another are created) nor was there appropriation and therefore no handling of stolen goods either. So therefore no offence was committed. This was plainly wrong so the gap in the TA68 caused by *Preddy* was filled that same year by the Theft (Amendment) Act 1996 which inserted in a rather pointed way a new section 15A into the old TA68 making it a specific offence to obtain a money transfer by deception.

Similarly, a builder who dishonestly over-bills for the work he has done is guilty of plain theft as soon as he pays the inflated cheque into his account, since that is theft of the overpayment from V's account. But bank accounts gave rise to issues: what if there was no money in the account or the withdrawal lay outside an agreed overdraft limit?

These – and other – loopholes have been cured by the Fraud Act 2006 which removes the need for deception but covers fraud through a false representation (section 2) or a failure to disclose information (s3) or through an abuse of position (s4) where D is a trustee, banker or solicitor, for example. Nor does there have to be an actual gain or loss.

Third, Crimes Leading To Crimes Or Which Are Committed With Others

These are crimes which are crimes because (1) they lead to crimes or (2) they are done with others. They include:

- Attempt, as in attempted murder, etc
- Accessory or accomplice to a crime
- Conspiracy with others to commit a crime
- Public order offences involving several people

This area of criminal law is not quite so obvious. It includes: planning a crime (even if the crime that was planned didn't happen); helping someone (D1) carry out a crime by being his accomplice (D2); and several Ds roaming round in a crowd (these are 'public order offences' with graphic names such as 'affray', 'violent disorder' and 'riot' which reflect increasing magnitudes of disturbance).

In the first (planning a crime), D doesn't have to get so far as committing the intended crime to be liable. D can **attempt** to commit the crime (doing acts more than merely preparatory to the commission of a crime). D can **conspire** with others to commit a crime (agree to commit a crime). D can **incite** others to commit a crime (encourage the commission of a crime). All of these are offences in their own right and are called **inchoate** ('just begun', 'undeveloped') crimes. In all of them the intended crime does not have to happen.

Whereas if D is charged with being an **accomplice** (helping, encouraging or causing the commission of a crime) the crime has to have taken place for D to be guilty (and D is said to have secondary liability, not being the principal protagonist in the commission of the crime). D must have done something which assisted D1, realising that what he did was capable of assisting and intending it would do so.

This may seem a rather unimportant and technical aspect of criminal law, but it's recently been one of the most debated. With an ageing population and limited public finances, the criminality of **assisted suicide** is being reconsidered. For instance, knowing whether or not your wife could go to prison if she helps you to travel to a Swiss euthanasia clinic can affect whether – or when – you decide to go. In practice, prosecutions aren't taken forward. But many people – and not just lawyers – for years have demanded that the law in this area have greater certainty.

Finally, Administrative Offences

Administrative offences are minor offences (for instance **driving offences** under the Road Traffic Act 1988 such as speeding and parking infringements) which rarely go to trial, usually attract fines not prison, and fall short of being regarded by society as criminal in the accepted sense.

Well, did you get all four in your list?

Whether or not you did, we've now covered the universe of criminal offences which I hope has given you a flavour of criminal law. But there's another area (which we'll touch on briefly):

Defences

D may have done the deed. But there may be circumstances exonerating D and negating criminal intent. These are **defences**. A successful defence means no crime has been committed.

There are all sorts of defences but the most common ones are: self defence (I did it but I had to), necessity / duress (I did it but I was made to) and disease of the mind or insanity (I did it but I couldn't help it or didn't know what I was doing). You may think that pleading insanity is a soft touch, but the sentence can be much longer than prison – and indeed for life – because D is 'detained at Her Majesty's pleasure' (which means for as long as the government likes) and is only let out when cured or no longer a potential menace.

Circumstances that don't amount to defences to a crime may still support a **plea in mitigation** which can reduce, and even remove the need to impose, a sentence. In other words, D is convicted, so has a criminal record, but the sentence may be reduced. So a plea in mitigation means a crime has been committed but the plea will be taken into account when sentencing (see Chapter 3).

Hard Cases

You may have noticed that cases can contradict each other. What a court says in one case may be different from what a court previously said. This happens more often than you might think. It's partly because the facts may be subtly different. Or because society has moved on. Far from being fixed forever like a fly in amber, the law is constantly changing, to keep up with changes in society and people's views of what is right and wrong, good and bad.

What the courts try to do when this happens is to **distinguish** one case from the other on the facts – in other words they say that contradictory judgments were arrived at because the facts of each case were different and led to different interpretations. This doesn't always work: sometimes cases are completely contradictory on the same facts. In which case the top court (which is now the Supreme Court) will simply come out and say so.

This may shock you. You may think the law should run along a straight track until Parliament changes the law through enacting legislation (called Acts of Parliament) from when it runs in a different direction until the next change, and so on. But that's not what happens. What happens is that judges make law when they apply old law to new facts, although this in itself is a contentious statement. One of the hotly debated issues in jurisprudence (roughly the philosophy of law) is whether judges do make new law and, if they do, whether they should. The argument against is that they are not elected and only the elected legislature (Parliament) has the constitutional right to make new law. See Chapters 10 and 11 on this.

So law students study **hard cases** where the decision was difficult or controversial or marked a change in the views of judges and society. *Caldwell* is an example of this. This is how the law develops. Of course, if all you are studying are hard cases you'll soon conclude that the law is a constantly evolving mess. Nicola Padfield, a noted criminal law academic (she's a don at Cambridge) as well as a criminal judge (she sits as a recorder, a type of judge, in the Crown Court) makes exactly this point in her textbook on criminal law: 'You may conclude that the criminal law is in …a state of chaos because, in studying criminal law, we often concentrate on the most difficult and controversial areas but courts up and down the country are today dealing with many criminal prosecutions with little difficulty.'

So there are large swathes of the law that don't change and aren't controversial. But that's not where law students spend their time. They spend their time on the hard cases. For lawyers in practice this isn't so – as a lawyer appearing in court you may only encounter a significant 'hard case' once or twice in your career (we'll see more of what lawyers actually do in Chapter 3).

In some respects criminal law itself is easy. It's easy to find: most of it is enshrined in different bits of legislation (laws passed by Parliament) and if the state doesn't like certain types of conduct it simply passes more laws to make them crimes. Nor is it difficult to grasp, at least in concept: criminal law identifies behaviours deemed unsavoury by society and discourages people from doing them by punishing those who do.

But what makes criminal law difficult is not what you find in the law books but the way it is applied and enforced by the police and the Crown Prosecution Service (CPS). The police catch alleged criminals and compile files of supporting evidence which they send to the CPS. The CPS reviews the files, decides whether a case should be brought (depending on the chances of winning) and, if so, prosecutes D.

The complexities lie around the decision to prosecute (which is why some apparent crimes aren't brought to book and other trivial ones seem to be) and which offence(s) to charge D with (often the law overlaps so allowing different, competing charges to be brought, which can be messy). A lot of it revolves around how strong the evidence is and whether it is admissible in court and this depends on a whole separate strand of law called the rules of evidence – as we shall see in Chapter 3.

But before we get there let's look at wrongs that aren't crimes.

CHAPTER 2

TORT

Criminal law – illegal – civil law – unlawful – tort – *Donoghue v Stevenson* – negligence – damages – duty of care – reasonably foreseeable – breach of the duty of care – nexus – causation – remoteness of damage – contributory negligence – novus actus interveniens – volenti non fit injuria – strict liability – trespass to the person – false imprisonment – defective products – vicarious liability – psychiatric injury – economic torts – Denning – economic loss – disclaimer – exclusion clause – breach of statutory duty – personal injury – defamation – libel – slander – product liability – professional indemnity – medical negligence – quantum – neighbour disputes

As we saw in the last chapter, criminal law is a set of rules imposed by the state to ensure that society is able to function. It bans and punishes (and so aims to prevent) conduct that would otherwise lead to a breakdown in everyday life. **Criminal law** bans conduct that is **illegal**. If found guilty, D will be sentenced, usually to a fine or gaol (the old-fashioned spelling of jail has been retained by lawyers since Norman times because of its frequency in legal documents).

Criminal v Civil Law

Civil law is different. **Civil law** is the set of rules provided by the state to enable citizens to regulate their dealings with each other ('civil' comes from the Latin 'civis' meaning citizen, as indeed does the word 'civilisation'). Civil law sets out our rights. If D infringes your rights, then that act of infringement is **unlawful** without necessarily being illegal: you can bring a claim against D but D won't end up in gaol; instead D will have to pay you compensation which in law is called damages. The state isn't directly involved in civil law except to provide a system of rules (law) governing relations between citizens and, when these break down, places (courts) where disputes can be decided by people (judges) qualified to settle them.

So all the state does under civil law is to lay down what the law is and to provide a mechanism for allowing citizens to bring cases against each other. In the past some civil wrongs were crimes – for instance, failure to pay a debt which is how Charles Dickens's dad ended up in gaol. But that's no longer the case unless the debt is in fact a fine resulting from a conviction for a crime (which makes sense as the money meant to be paid is to avoid prison in the first place). It's true that a criminal act may give rise to civil liability (D may go to gaol for hitting V but V may bring a claim against D for damages too). However, it's rare since most criminals are not worth suing because they're broke, which is often why they are criminals (instead victims of crime can seek recompense from the Criminal Injuries Compensation Board). So it's best to keep criminal and civil separate in your own mind. In fact, having done criminal in the last chapter, from here on in everything else in this book is civil (the law between citizens, if you like).

Tort

The area of civil law which is about wrongs which fall short of being criminal acts has a strange name: **tort**. It's from the French for 'wrong'. But although tort is French, lawyers don't pronounce it in the French way with a silent second 't' ('tore') but so it sounds like 'taught'.

My starting point for tort is a snail in a bottle. Little did this poor snail know that it was going to star posthumously in what is possibly the single most important case in modern legal history.

Back in 1932 there wasn't much by way of consumer legislation. So when a woman bought a bottle of pop from a shop, drank it, discovered the remains of a decomposing snail at the bottom and fell ill, her only source of redress was against the person who'd sold her the bottle (the shopkeeper). Only it wasn't his fault. He hadn't put the snail in the bottle. The manufacturer had. But the woman (I'll call her C for claimant) didn't have a contract (a legally binding agreement) with the manufacturer. She only had a contract with the shopkeeper. So she had no right of redress.

This was patently unfair, so the House of Lords said C could sue the manufacturer because the manufacturer had a duty of care to consumers of its drinks. It knew people would buy its products to drink (why else was it in business?) so it had a duty to supply drinks that weren't contaminated by decomposing snails – even though it might not be under a direct contractual obligation to the consumers.

This case, **Donoghue v Stevenson**, was in effect the start of the modern law of **negligence**. And negligence lies at the heart of tort.

Before the Industrial Revolution there was little sense of social obligation to make reparation for harm caused casually and unintentionally. If you got hurt or injured, that was life, and it wasn't valued greatly (besides, the rich land-owning classes were less exposed to these risks than the great unwashed). The exception was if there was a 'special relationship' for instance between a surgeon and patient or a carriage driver and the passenger. Gradually these individual special duties were replaced by a single principle that there is a duty to make reparation where injury is inflicted by the failure to take due care. This failure to take due care is what the law calls 'negligence'. And *Donoghue v Stevenson* is a key case. Since then negligence has developed through case law into a tightly defined concept.

NEGLIGENCE

Let's imagine that I'm up a ladder repairing my roof. You're walking along the pavement. I drop a hammer and it hits you on the toe. In order for you to sue me successfully you need to establish a number of things:

- That I shouldn't have dropped the hammer
- That I should have foreseen that pedestrians would be walking under my ladder
- That the hammer did hit you
- That you did suffer injury
- That the injury was the result of the hammer hitting you

If you succeed in establishing all of that, then I should recompense you by paying you **damages** (the legal term for monetary compensation).

Did I Drop The Hammer Carelessly?

The way the law frames this is to ask whether I should have been taking care as I was using the hammer. In other words, did I owe a **duty of care** and, if so, to whom? The answer is: yes; I owe a duty of care to others around me.

Should I Have Foreseen That You'd Be Below?

This boils down to asking: was it **reasonably foreseeable** that a pedestrian (you), might be walking under or near my ladder? Again, the answer is: yes. That's what pavements are for, for pedestrians to use. So it was reasonably foreseeable that someone might be walking along the pavement while I was working on my roof.

Did The Hammer Hit You?

Yes, evidently, but actually what the law wants to know is: was the fact the hammer hit you a direct result of the **breach of the duty of care** I owed you? In other words, is there a link, a connection – what lawyers call a **nexus**. Answer: yes. In legal terms it's called **causation**: the breach of duty caused the injury.

Did You Suffer Injury As A Result?

You did. Being hit by the hammer caused the bruised toe. But the technical test the law applies is: was that bruising a reasonably foreseeable consequence of the accident? Sometimes some apparent consequences are too remote. So this test is called **remoteness of damage**.

Now, if we go back and recast those questions, they look something like this:

- That I should have foreseen that pedestrians would be below

  = did I owe you a duty of care? (existence of duty of care)

- That I dropped the hammer carelessly

  = did I breach that duty? (breach of that duty of care)

- That the hammer I dropped hit you

  = causation: breach of duty caused the accident

- That you suffered injury as a result

  = remoteness of damage: the injury you suffered was a reasonably foreseeable consequence of the accident.

So negligence requires a duty of care, breach of that duty and damage caused by that breach (this damage not to be too remote from the breach).

Wagon Mound No 1

Remoteness of damage can itself throw up legal issues and arguments. In a case called *Wagon Mound No 1,* a stevedore (dock worker) was unloading cargo from a boat (the Wagon Mound). He negligently dropped a plank, it caused a spark, the spark caused a fire, the fire lit the boat and the boat set light to the whole of Sydney harbour. Which, told like that, makes it sound quite funny but I'm sure at the time it wasn't.

The question was not one of duty of care or breach of duty, but one of causation and remoteness. Was it reasonably foreseeable that if you dropped a plank you might burn down a whole harbour? The court (which was trying to allocate the cost of rebuilding the harbour) said basically that it wasn't so unforeseeable that the stevedore's firm couldn't be liable. The loss was one of degree. It was a fire all right. It just happened to be a damned great big one.

Contributory Negligence

Now let's get back to the hammer accident. Suppose I had put a sign up saying 'workman above' and you disregarded that and walked right under the ladder (which proved unlucky for you). I might admit liability but then counter-argue that you shouldn't have walked directly under the ladder given my warning sign. Now there's a lot of law about warning signs (we'll encounter them in a case called *Thornton v Shoe Lane Parking* and also under Occupiers' Liability in the chapter on property law later on) but for now I just want to focus on whether by your act of walking under my ladder you contributed to the accident.

This is called **contributory negligence**: you contributed to the damage you suffered. The court will assess as a percentage how much what you did contributed to the accident (say 30%) and reduce the damages accordingly (so I pay you 70% not 100% of the damages awarded).

Let's say something else happened instead. Suppose the hammer falls, doesn't hit you but in trying to avoid it you step out in the road and are hit by a passing cyclist. In court I might argue **novus actus interveniens** ('new action intervening' – the same idea as in the last chapter) – meaning that my act wasn't the cause of your injury but a subsequent, supervening act which may reduce (or in some cases remove) my liability.

There are some cases where, basically, if someone takes a risk it is their fault. If someone, for example, volunteers to be a human cannonball shot from a circus cannon and it goes wrong, then they've only got themselves to blame: they volunteered to take on the risk. This is called **volenti non fit injuria** (which means loosely: injury is not made by willingness, that is, if you volunteered there isn't an injury).

Now, just to show you how it all connects, do you remember that in the last chapter we talked about manslaughter by gross negligence? You can now begin to see that the criminal offence has similar ingredients to tort since D owes V a duty of care, breaches that duty and does so recklessly (not caring about the consequences or so carelessly that this is the effect). And in those rare cases where the criminal law imposes liability for omissions, it's because there's a special duty of care owed, for instance, by the parent to the child or the carer to the elderly and infirm relative. So the state intervenes to punish D. These cross-connections between two areas of law (crime and tort) will either please you as they show the richness, fluidity and complexity of the law or freak you out. As a student I was freaked out by them: I just wanted to know what the law was so I could pass my assessments; now I find it enriching to spot these things.

STRICT LIABILITY

So that's a snapshot of negligence which turns on D being at fault in some way for breach of a duty of care he owed C. D did something that he wouldn't have done if he had been taking reasonable care (because if I had been taking *reasonable care* I would not have been in breach of the *duty of care* which I owed you and other pedestrians when I was using my hammer).

However there are some types of tort which are known as no-fault torts: I'm liable regardless of whether or not I was careless. This is called **strict liability**. Now I don't want to confuse you by drawing a comparison with criminal law which is completely different. But you'll know from the last chapter that there is some sense of 'fault' required (for instance in murder). The same in the main is true of most torts. But there are some crimes where intention or state of mind is irrelevant (such as speeding, parking on a yellow line, dropping litter and other offences which although strictly speaking criminal are nowadays regarded as administrative violations). The same is true of torts of strict liability. Funnily enough the oldest torts were like this, including trespass.

Trespass

Trespass is usually associated with land. You've probably come across signs saying: 'Trespassers Will Be Prosecuted'. Lawyers find this funny (there's not much to laugh about in the law). The joke is that people only get prosecuted for crimes and trespass is not a crime but a civil wrong (a tort). So to say that trespassers (civil wrong) will be prosecuted (criminal offence) is, well, wrong. If it said: Trespassers Will Be Sued, that would be correct, if a little less intimidating.

Anyway, I didn't bring you all this way to tell you that (besides, we'll return to trespass to land when we do land law). Rather, that there's something called **trespass to the person** that can be committed by the merest touch. It can include an unwanted kiss, an unasked-for haircut and the wrong chemical dye applied to your hair – *Nash v Sheen* (1953). It can also include the fear of trespass, such as silent phone calls from a stalker. These may remind you of criminal law: battery being the touch; and the fear of it being assault. In fact, back in the mists of time, trespass was a crime. So the reference to prosecuting trespassers isn't quite so daft after all.

There's another type of trespass to the person called **false imprisonment**. But this doesn't mean kidnapping someone or keeping them in a dungeon. It means simply preventing someone from moving in a particular direction. (Although, somewhat hilariously, someone who was trapped in a public toilet through a defective lock failed in their action for false imprisonment against the local authority because there was no direct contact, so therefore no false imprisonment – *Sayers v Harlow UDC* (1958). Not hilarious for the person inconvenienced, I hasten to add.)

Trespass, in these various forms, is said to be 'actionable *per se*' (actionable in itself) meaning that provided it happens there doesn't have to be any fault on D's part.

Two other examples of torts of strict liability worth mentioning are: tortious liability for **defective products** (where defective goods cause harm to the public); and employer's **vicarious liability** (which makes an employer – or his insurance company – liable for wrongful acts by his employees in the course of their work; 'vicarious' because the employer is made liable at one remove by the employee's act).

This latter is important because it enables an employee (E1) to sue an employer for injury caused to him or her (E1) by another employee (E2) during the course of employment. It means E1 is more likely to be able to recover something, for instance from the employer's insurer.

TORTS WHERE DAMAGE IS INTANGIBLE

You will have gathered so far that tort is at heart about actual damage. Indeed, if you haven't suffered any actual loss or injury, there is nothing to be compensated for. So, if when I dropped the hammer, you were wearing steel-capped boots and didn't suffer any injury, you would have nothing to claim compensation for. Indeed, for a long time it was thought that you had to have suffered actual damage (physical damage to an object, for instance if the boots themselves were damaged, or physical injury to the person) to be able to claim at all.

The modern law of tort is not quite like that any more. I want to pick out two areas where it has developed significantly. One is in the area of **psychiatric injury** (including what is called nervous shock). The other is **economic torts** that cause purely pecuniary damage (aka economic loss).

Psychiatric Injury

One of the most famous judgments ever begins: 'It was bluebell time in Kent' and goes on to describe a horrific crash in which a family was almost wiped out when a car left the road and careered into them. The family – two adults and several children – had gone out into the countryside to pick bluebells. They parked by the side of the road and all bar the mother crossed the road to the bluebells on the other side. When a passing car ran off the road, killing or maiming them, the mother witnessed it all from her side of the road. She suffered what in those days (1970) was called 'nervous shock' but which we would now describe as trauma of the deepest sort. Problem: she didn't suffer any physical damage or injury. And in those days that's what you needed in order to be able to claim.

The judge in this case (*Hinz v Berry*) was Lord Denning, one of the most famous judges of the last hundred years. **Denning** was Hampshire born and bred and always affected a country burr when he spoke to make people think he was a bit of a yokel, simple and unworldly.

Ha. It was all an act.

Denning had a razor sharp mind. He'd got a first in maths at Oxford then switched to law and got a first in that. He was a total iconoclast and rebel, even more striking because he was a judge, and beloved of the common man for manipulating the law to achieve what he felt was the just outcome. Lawyers and other judges hated this because it made the law unpredictable – though exciting.

Denning was promoted to the House of Lords (where there were five judges) but took a demotion to the Court of Appeal (where there are three) because he felt he could do more good if he was up against two rather than four. Which is why the recent history of English law is littered with cases he decided that changed the law fundamentally. *Hinz v Berry* is one.

I imagine that, like a lot of accidents involving vehicles, there was an insurance company lurking in the background and Denning was going to make damn sure it paid up, regardless of what its silver-tongued lawyers might argue. He was that kind of judge. And so he did. He basically extended causation to include damage caused other than by direct injury.

The judgment is also famous because of the language Denning used. At a time when judges droned on using long words in long sentences (and lots of Latin, natch), his judgments used short words and pithy sentences. They were like staccato bursts of machine-gun fire. Utterly brilliant. He'll be popping up later.

Hinz v Berry prompted the development of a complex area of law. The courts have had to circumscribe the nature of the tort otherwise anyone reading about a bad accident in the paper could claim to suffer some psychiatric reaction or illness as a result. The courts have by and large said that:

(1)   the reaction (which must be a provable medical condition) has to flow either from fear for one's own safety or that of others close to one (such as family members or close friends); and

(2)   there must be close proximity in terms of place and time between the incident affecting the family member and the person suffering the reaction.

This was established by a case (*Alcock v South Yorks*) arising out of the Hillsborough football tragedy in 1989 when 96 Liverpool fans were crushed at Sheffield Wednesday's stadium through poor crowd control. That case was brought against the South Yorkshire police service. Other cases such as *White v South Yorks* and *Frost v South Yorks* were brought by members of the police service for trauma they too suffered.

It followed from this case that watching the disaster unfold live on TV (as in fact happened) would satisfy (2) above but reading about it in the paper wouldn't. In a subsequent case involving the Piper Alpha oil rig disaster in the North Sea, a 'mere bystander' who wasn't otherwise involved (unlike, say, a rescuer) was unable to claim (*McFarlane v EE Caledonia* (1994)).

Economic Loss

The other tortious area I want to mention in passing concerns what is called pure **economic loss**. Financial loss flowing from injury to person or damage to property has always been recoverable. But it took a long time for the courts to be prepared to award damages for pure economic loss – that is, financial loss in the absence of actual injury to person or damage to property.

For many years, economic torts (as they are called) were limited. The courts feared 'the floodgates would open' meaning that loads of cases would follow for unimaginably enormous losses. So the courts required evidence of what they saw as deliberate wrongdoing (virtually amounting to fraud or sharp practice).

Then in 1964 the case of *Hedley Byrne v Heller* established that negligence could apply to statements: provided D (defendant) had special expertise in the topic giving rise to the statement, and C (claimant) relied on the statement (and it was reasonable for C to do so), then any loss C suffered was recoverable from D.

The case arose in the context of a bank reference given by D for one of its customers which C relied on, meaning there was no actual contract between C and D that C could claim compensation under (we do contract later). So instead C had to claim against D in tort (like *Donoghue v Stevenson*). But there was no actual injury or damage as such. It was pure economic loss. Yet C won. This meant that if, say, a stockbroker gave a share tip at a party, did so negligently and it was wrong, he could be sued even though he'd given the tip in a social context (provided, of course, that it was reasonable for C to have relied on it in those circumstances).

Three years later, the Misrepresentation Act 1967 widened things beyond the area of special expertise: C can claim damages (in the tort of misrepresentation) for economic loss due to negligent as well as fraudulent (deliberate) untrue statements made by D if they led to C entering into a contract with D. But C still needs to form a contract with D after the negligence in order to claim; the floodgates aren't yet open.

The Language Of Tort

A few final bits & pieces before we wrap up the law of tort.

These are some other terms linked to tort which you might hear lawyers using:

Disclaimer – this is a sentence or short paragraph drafted by a company's lawyers and written on its products or property, to try to exclude liability. (In a contract, it's known as an **exclusion clause**.) It says that you can't claim against the company for injury or damage to property. But Parliament has passed statutes to make some of these disclaimers ineffective, particularly for consumers (for example, where the company has been negligent or someone has died as a result).

Breach of statutory duty – some legislation imposes a duty of care, for instance on local authorities in certain circumstances, so allowing an individual to claim for the tort of breach of statutory duty.

EXAMPLES OF TORT IN PRACTICE

Personal Injury

The most common **personal injury** cases concern tripping on defective pavements for which the local authority is usually liable in negligence. Lawyers who do this work are sometimes labelled 'ambulance chasers', the idea being that they follow ambulances to hospitals to encourage patients to sue for compensation if they are there as a result of some injury. This can encourage a claims culture where everyone sees themselves as a victim and the cost to society rises inexorably.

Defamation

The tort of **defamation** (impugning someone's reputation) has been around for centuries. Even though it might seem to you and me as if it's about intangible damage (and so therefore should be recent), I imagine that reputation may have mattered even more in the past when communities were smaller and closer, so what neighbours thought of you was much more important in terms of your social standing, status in the community, the wellbeing of your family and your professional success. So the tort of defamation is long-established and remains one of the most visible: it makes front-page news (not least since the newspapers are so often the culprit). Defamation divides into **libel** and **slander**. Libel is what is written. Slander is what is said. Libel lawyers tend to be found in law firms specialising in media law, which we'll come to later.

Other Examples

Product liability is an aspect of tort and involves representing companies accused of it (big manufacturers such as car makers, for instance) or consumers who have suffered as a result of defective products. It often involves 'class actions' (imported from the US) where one law firm will act for hundreds of individuals all suing the same company for the same thing in one big court case rather than each of them having to bring a separate claim on his or her own.

Professional indemnity is another aspect of tort, involving advice given negligently by professionals such as accountants, surveyors and solicitors. These professionals carry professional indemnity insurance, as it's called, which means they (and their firms) are personally covered. Hence the term. There are law firms that specialise in defending professionals against such claims.

Medical negligence is a specialist area of tort law and is about suing healthcare providers for failing to meet adequate standards of service provision, for instance if a surgical procedure goes wrong. The most harrowing cases involve children severely damaged in childbirth. Much of the law is about assessing liability (whether anyone is liable) and **quantum** (the level of damages to be awarded). In the case of children the damages can run to millions of pounds to provide for their care for the rest of their lives. Again, there are lawyers and law firms that specialise in bringing such claims.

Neighbour disputes are a combination of tort and property which we'll explore later in the chapter on land law.

Which Leads Us To...

All of the above involve bringing or defending claims that may end up in court. This sort of work is known as dispute resolution or litigation and the lawyers who do it are known as litigators, as we shall see in the next chapter.

CHAPTER 3

LAW IN PRACTICE: COURTS

Accused – crime – defendant – prosecution – not guilty – convicted –
sentenced – criminal record – criminal case – magistrates' courts –
Crown Court – trial by jury – Old Bailey – civil case – claimant – claim –
county courts – High Court – Royal Courts of Justice – appellate system –
Court of Appeal – Supreme Court – burden of proof – beyond reasonable
doubt – balance of probabilities – prosecuted – acquitted – sued – claim –
inadmissible – rule of evidence – hearsay rule – cross-examination –
summary offences – indictable offences – judge – jury – offences triable
either way – matrimonial – personal injury – employment – consumer
cases – debt collection – construction – shipping – alternative dispute
resolution (ADR) – arbitration – mediation – expert determination – non-
contentious – contentious – without prejudice – settlement – letter before
claim – with respect – White Book – Green Book – Woolf – refresher –
disclosure – enforcement – payment into court – expert evidence –
mitigation – life sentence – parole – penology – recidivism – contempt of
court – damages – liquidated damages – penalties – punitive damages –
injunction – injunctive relief – restitution – rescission – enforce – court
order – ex parte – summary judgment – costs – solicitors – barristers –
sole practitioner – law firms – partnerships – chambers – sets –
advocates – litigators – litigation – instructions to counsel – brief – higher
rights of audience – avocats – conseils juridiques – fused legal profession
– attorney – trial attorneys – conferences with counsel – Bar – barristers'
clerk – clerk to the court – called to the Bar – pupillage – pupil master –
tenancy – Queen's Counsel (QC) – taking silk – juniors – legal aid –
human rights – immigration – housing – Citizens Advice Bureau

I want to ram home the distinction between criminal and civil law so I'm going to do it in the way that I hope will make most sense to you: court cases. Most people associate the law with TV programmes in which opposing lawyers put arguments to a judge and jury. Those cases are criminal (juries don't sit in civil cases).

The person **accused** of the alleged **crime** is called the **defendant** and the act of bringing the case against him or her is called a **prosecution** (the term 'prosecution' also applies to the 'prosecuting authority' – usually the Crown Prosecution Service). If the defendant is cleared he or she is said to be **not guilty**. If the case goes against him or her, they are **convicted** and are **sentenced** (the court determines the penalty). This penalty becomes part of their **criminal record**.

A **criminal case** is brought by the Crown (that is, the monarch – you remember R in the first chapter) against the defendant D before either the **magistrates' courts** (for less serious offences) or the **Crown Court** (for more serious offences – it's in the latter that you get **trial by jury**). The biggest criminal cases or those of greatest public interest go to the **Old Bailey** in London.

By contrast a **civil case** is brought by one citizen (the **claimant**) against another (also the defendant) and is a **claim** for damages. Civil cases are heard in the **county courts** and the **High Court**. The biggest go to the **Royal Courts of Justice** in the Strand (just down the street from the Old Bailey – it's why all the barristers' chambers and a lot of solicitors' firms are in that central part of London). You get judges and juries in criminal cases but judges on their own in civil cases.

In either case there is an appeal system (called the **appellate system**) so that if a party is not happy with the outcome they can get the case heard (decided) higher up by a more senior court. The appellate system is fused: that's to say, at the highest levels the same court hears both civil and criminal appeals because these are almost always on points of law so you want the top judges involved: the highest of which are the **Court of Appeal** and from there up to the **Supreme Court** (which has replaced the House of Lords as the top court as I'll explain later).

This fairly simple explanation is not the complete truth. Like the law itself, the court system is higgledy-piggledy with all sorts of small, specialist courts around the place. And whether or not someone can appeal can be complicated. But it will do for now (it's part of the dreaded English Legal System stuff I referred to in the introduction and I'll be coming back to it).

Now, let's get back to that case. In order for the jury to have found D guilty they must have been pretty sure he'd done it. But how sure?

Burden Of Proof

That is down to what is called the **burden of proof** (what the side bringing the case has to prove in order to win).

In criminal cases (which is what we have here) the prosecution must make its case that D is guilty **beyond reasonable doubt**. That means the court (magistrates, judge and jury, whoever) must believe beyond (a reasonable) doubt that D is guilty in order to convict. In short they need to be pretty certain.

But in a civil case the burden of proof is lower. Here the claimant C must establish his or her case on a **balance of probabilities**. As the word 'balance' suggests, this is much more a weighing up of the evidence on either side and if, on balance, the weight of evidence and strength of case favours C rather than D, it's C who wins.

As you can see, the burden of proof in criminal cases is higher. This is because criminal cases have greater gravity of consequence (punishment, even possibly prison, and a criminal record) so the court had better be pretty sure that D deserves it.

The most graphic example of this in recent times was the OJ Simpson case in the States. He was **prosecuted** and **acquitted** of murdering his wife: the (criminal) burden of proof wasn't met. So her family **sued** him (they made a civil **claim** against him effectively for the same alleged act) and won damages from him: the (civil) burden of proof was satisfied.

So, for a crime, it has to be beyond reasonable doubt (you have to be pretty sure he did it) and under civil law it's not as onerous: you have to prove D is liable on a balance of probabilities (you have to think it's 'more likely than not').

Rules Of Evidence

If D is found to be guilty, the court will need to consider what sentence to impose. This depends in part on D's criminal record – what he has done before. At that point – but only at that point – are D's previous convictions brought to the court's attention.

But I know what you're thinking.

Why aren't D's *previous* convictions used by the prosecution in *this* case? Why can they be mentioned *only after* D has been convicted this time, and only in order to help the judge impose the appropriate sentence? Surely the fact that D has committed (similar) crimes before is highly relevant to whether he has done so this time, since at the very least it shows a propensity to do so?

You're right. But that isn't good enough for the law. None of that tells you whether D *actually* did it this time. This will depend on what witnesses actually saw. You see, previous convictions are **inadmissible** as evidence in a criminal case. This is because of a famous **rule of evidence** called the **hearsay rule**. Understand this and I swear you will love the law.

Hearsay is just that: what you've heard someone else say; rather than what you have seen someone do. There are lots of rules surrounding what you can and can't use in court and when you're new to this they can seem pretty weird until you realise one thing: what the court is trying is *this* case. So the fact that D did something like it before is irrelevant (even if it demonstrates a tendency to do so). The fact that D already has a criminal record is irrelevant (even if it shows a criminal bent). The fact that someone might have heard someone else say that D did it is equally irrelevant.

In short, imagine this case is being tried in complete isolation from what D has done or not done at any time in the past.

Evidence has to be first-hand. It's no good witness A being called to give evidence if he says, 'B told me that the defendant D did it'. That would be hearsay. Instead the court would want to hear from B in person so that B can be questioned about why he thinks D did it and that allegation can be refuted by D.

There are similar rules about the police having to keep contemporaneous records of events. And rules about the extraction of confessions under duress. Ditto about the use of paid informers and grasses (crooks that are let off if they provide evidence to convict other crooks). Like journalists, the police rely on sources for information, and it's the veracity of those sources that gets questioned in court. However, over the years, the rule against hearsay has been relaxed. There are now many exceptions, often to do with what is and isn't admissible in documentary form (such as computer records) and wiretaps.

Police procedurals on TV have become more accurate. In the old days the copper would tell the villain: 'Anything you say may be taken down and used in evidence against you' which is wrong. It isn't 'against you' but just 'taken down' because whether that evidence is prejudicial to the defendant depends entirely on the circumstances of the case as it unfolds.

And because the burden of proof in a criminal case is, as mentioned, beyond reasonable doubt, the prosecution must present evidence that even after **cross-examination** of witnesses by the defence is enough for the jury (in a Crown Court case) to be pretty certain of the defendant's guilt.

I Did It, Guv

You may have heard that lawyers defending someone accused of a crime never want to know whether or not D 'did' it. Whether he did it – in a legal sense – depends on the definition of the crime so he may be wrong anyway. And, even if D has said he did it, there may be extenuating factors amounting to a defence.

But the real reason is that if D really did do it and tells his lawyer, the lawyer can't argue to the court that D didn't. This is because solicitors in the UK are 'officers of the Supreme Court'. They are part of the justice system. If they know a crime has been committed, they can't pervert justice by hiding it. So the lawyer must try to persuade the client to tell the truth in court. (The lawyer can't tell the court because anything a client tells a lawyer is confidential, unless the client says otherwise.) But if D won't tell the court, then the lawyer must stop working on the case. D will need to find another lawyer. So a lawyer never wants to know whether his client 'did it'. That's for the court (judge and jury) to decide, having heard all of the evidence on both sides.

Criminal Courts

Having started with a case involving a jury, I have to admit that 95% of criminal cases don't involve a jury at all. They are tried in magistrates' courts. These are for the least serious offences, known as **summary offences**.

You may be surprised to know that the majority of magistrates aren't lawyers; they aren't even professional judges, but volunteers (often called JPs or justices of the peace). They sit in benches of three and are advised by a court clerk, justices' clerk or legal adviser. The exception is in London and other major cities, where there may be professional judges called district judges (once known as stipendiary magistrates) who are lawyers and they sit on their own rather than in threes.

More serious cases (known as **indictable offences**) are heard before the Crown Court with a **judge** (called a circuit judge) and a **jury**. There are some inbetween offences (**offences triable either way**) which will be tried before a magistrates' court unless D asks to be tried before the Crown Court. D may do this if he thinks a jury may be more sympathetic than magistrates or a judge sitting on their own.

Juries represent the popular conception of the law as it appears in court. But they are only used in criminal cases and only then in Crown Courts where only 5% of criminal offences are heard. The bulk of criminal offences (including all those involving young people) are heard in magistrates' courts (in the latter case sitting as the youth court where the rules of procedure are less strict).

Civil Courts

By contrast the bulk of civil cases are heard in what are called county courts before circuit judges (named after the fact that originally judges went round the country in circuits, so each place would be visited three or four times a year in what were called quarterly assizes). However, major cases (anything worth over £15,000) are heard in the High Court.

We know what criminal cases involve: all of the stuff mentioned in Chapter 1. But what about civil cases?

Examples Of Civil Cases

Well, these will involve claims for tortious liability (see Chapter 2) and, for individuals, **matrimonial** cases (people getting divorced and arguing over who gets what including custody of the kids), **personal injury** (tripping over pavements, being hit by falling hammers, etc, etc), **employment** (when someone is sacked or made redundant they may want to sue their employer) and **consumer cases** (such as the snail in the bottle), most of which are for breach of contract (which we'll cover later). Some cases involve businesses pursuing individuals for non-payment of money that's due, which is called **debt collection**.

However, the bulk of civil cases are brought by businesses against each other. Disputes are almost endemic in business. Some of the biggest commercial disputes concern:

Construction and engineering involving big building projects. This is a highly specialised area in its own right for two reasons: first, the terminology and jargon of the construction industry require specialist knowledge; second, almost all construction contracts lead to some form of litigation (that is, the parties end up in disagreement and go to court).

Shipping traditionally involves disputes about the use of ships to carry cargo (known as dry shipping) and disputes over collisions between ships (called wet shipping or admiralty). Both have their own terminology. So salvage concerns the rights of those who rescue cargo (and the wreck itself) when a ship sinks, while freight is the charge for carrying goods. And a bill of lading is evidence of the contract of carriage, is receipt for the goods, and evidence of title to the goods being shipped. These types of dispute are often international involving parties from around the world. London has historically been a popular place to bring such claims because the courts are regarded as above corruption and English law is relatively clear.

Alternative Dispute Resolution

Going to court is not the only way to resolve disputes. Since it is notoriously slow and expensive, methods of **alternative dispute resolution** (or **ADR** as it's called) have sprung up. These include:

Arbitration – originally a more flexible, simpler and cheaper way of getting a dispute resolved by having it heard by a qualified arbitrator, but now with its own set of rules and run by a number of international arbitral bodies, such as the ICC (the International Chamber of Commerce International Court of Arbitration) in Paris. Crucially, both parties must have previously agreed to arbitration for it to happen. Used in big, international construction, shipping and commercial disputes.

Mediation – where the parties appoint a mediator who will talk to each party individually and try to help them work out an agreed way of solving a dispute. This is often used by individuals involved in divorce who are trying to agree what is best for their children; and by businesses that have continuing dealings with each other.

Expert determination – where the two parties will simply appoint an expert to decide between them. This is often used in disputes as wide-ranging as engineering and publishing where both parties want, and will trust, an expert who understands their industry or profession and so will be able to grasp the intricacies of their dispute.

Now, a word of warning. I've listed above certain areas of law that are prone to litigation. But for every area of law there are always cases arising out of it. So as I mention more and more areas of specialist law I want you to realise that each one, even if it is **non-contentious** (not about going to court), will have a **contentious** side to it (it can give rise to cases in court). I'll come back to this later so don't worry if what I've just said isn't all that clear.

The Language Of Civil Litigation

There are certain terms you will come across in litigation:

Without prejudice – this is what solicitors put at the top of letters in which they are making an offer of money to end the dispute (a **settlement**) to the other side. You don't want your offer to be rejected and then for it to be brought up in court to show that your case is weak (why would you be seeking a settlement otherwise, so the argument might go). And you're not admitting any fault. So the words 'without prejudice' mean just that. The courts allow this because they want disputes resolved. And the sooner they're resolved the better (and cheaper).

People who aren't lawyers often get fixated with the term and use it in letters where actually you don't want it to appear. For example, if you are writing a **letter before claim** (as part of the court process you have to give the other side a final chance to settle before you issue a formal claim against them) you don't want that to be 'without prejudice' because that's as if the letter didn't exist, which rather defeats the purpose.

With respect – often heard in court when a barrister is addressing a judge. It means: 'I think you are talking hogwash'. So when a barrister says to a judge: 'With respect, m'lud' (m'lud = 'my lord', is pronounced 'mer-ladd' and is the usual way of addressing a judge), it means 'I completely disagree with what you have just said'.

And 'm'learned friend' (pronounced 'mer-learn-id-friend') is what a barrister calls the barrister on the other side. It is such a small world that barristers tend to know each other and be good friends even if they are forever beating each other up in court. But sometimes tempers flare. Calling each other 'm'learned friend' helps maintain decorum in court.

White Book – not a set of witch's spells but a big thick book (which, yes, does have white covers) containing all of the rules of procedure which govern the way High Court cases are run. The **Green Book** is the equivalent for county courts.

Woolf – the extensive set of reforms devised in the 1990s by Lord Woolf, a distinguished judge, to make the civil court system faster and cheaper.

Refresher – a type of fee paid to barristers to be retained on a case.

Disclosure – when each side in a civil case shows their evidence to the other side (previously known as discovery). You might think this odd – why would you want to reveal your hand like that? The answer is that the court cannot arrive at a fair determination if one side can ambush the other with evidence or an argument that the other side hasn't had time to consider.

Enforcement – what the winning side does when it has obtained a judgment against the losing side and wants to get hold of the money owed, usually involving bailiffs to recover the damages and costs awarded.

Payment into court – a sum that D pays into court by way of an offer of settlement. Then if the other side fails to win more by going to trial they end up paying the costs of both parties. Why? Because the court says the other side should have accepted D's offer, ended the dispute and saved time and costs.

Expert evidence – where an expert not involved in the dispute is called by either or both parties to provide evidence on an area outside the court's own knowledge, to help the court: anything from medical to geological, from firearms and explosives to shipping and aircraft.

Penalties (Criminal) And Remedies (Civil)

What is the result of going (or being taken) to court?

Penalties – Criminal

In criminal cases, D is sentenced and thereafter has a criminal record. But before D is sentenced he is allowed to put in a plea in **mitigation** ('mitigation' means any argument that will persuade the court to pass a more lenient sentence). Some crimes carry a mandatory **life sentence** which means that D has to be given the sentence of life imprisonment. But life doesn't mean life. D is eligible for **parole** after a period provided he or she has behaved well in prison and shows remorse (is sorry).

There is a whole academic branch of study called **penology** – a cross between law and sociology – which looks at whether prison works and, in particular, the rate of **recidivism** (convicted criminals committing further crimes when they come out). It also looks at the purposes of prison: punishment; deterrence (to stop others doing it); keeping criminals off the streets (to make society a safer place); or reform (to turn criminals into law-abiding citizens) – probably a bit of all four. In Roman times parricides (killers of their own dads – presumably so common they had a name for it) were sewn into a sack along with an animal menagerie comprising a dog, a cock, a viper and – not much room left for this one – an ape, all of them alive. The sack was then chucked into the sea. Fun. We'll be coming back to the Romans in a bit.

Prison is very rarely used for civil wrongs. In Dickens's day it was used for debtors (which is what happened to his dad, scarring Dickens for life). Nowadays if someone consistently flouts or ignores a civil judgment the court may eventually treat that as **contempt of court** for which the court can send D to gaol, though not for long.

Remedies – Civil

There are a host of remedies – as they are called – open to a claimant in civil proceedings. The most obvious is **damages** (money) which is designed, in the case of tort, to put you (back) in the position you would have been in if the tort hadn't happened; and, in the case of contract, to put you (forward) in the position you would have been in if the contract had been properly performed. That sounds complicated but all it means is that the court will generally try to put you in the same position as if whatever went wrong hadn't happened.

In the case of contracts you may encounter **liquidated damages** (sums specified in the contract to be the cost of non-performance). But **penalties** (sums designed to look like compensation but meant to act as deterrents and penalise) are not allowed. In tort it is possible to seek **punitive damages** but not triple damages as they have in the US.

Loss of life and limb have specific calculations attached to them: there are entire law books devoted to the relevant formulae.

There are other types of relief. C can seek an **injunction** (aka **injunctive relief**) to stop something from happening, **restitution** to have something returned or **rescission** to have the contract treated as ended.

Of course, it's one thing winning in court and quite another getting any money out of D. Once C has a court order she has to **enforce** it which can be a whole other set of legal proceedings in its own right.

There's not much point in suing someone if they are going to move all of their assets offshore before you can enforce against them so there are some types of **court order** you can get in advance (such as search and seizure orders and asset freezing orders). In these cases you don't want D to know what you are doing, otherwise he'll move the money anyway. So these orders tend to be obtained **ex parte** (pronounced 'x-party', meaning 'from the one party') which means C applies to the court, without D knowing. Obviously this means the court hears just one side of the story, so it has to be very sure that C is in the right to grant an ex parte order.

It is also possible to obtain **summary judgment** where C's claim is so watertight, so open-and-shut, that the court will grant judgment there and then without having to go to a full trial.

Costs

A lot of what parties do during litigation is driven by **costs**.

Litigation is expensive, so C will need to think about:

- The value and importance of the claim (how much does what happened matter? how much will it cost her?)
- The time involved (keeping and finding records, talking to lawyers and appearing in court as a witness on the day – it can be a long and complicated process to take a case all the way to a trial in one of the higher courts)
- The likelihood of winning (there's no such thing in real life as a cast iron case: there's always a chance C might lose)

And it's part of a lawyer's job to make sure C is aware of all of this. Judges don't like people wasting either the court's time or their money on big legal bills for no good reason.

Litigation Lawyers

Now we've looked at the courts and examples of cases brought before them, I want to introduce you to the lawyers that do this type of work. You probably already know one type: barristers.

But, in fact, just stepping back from purely litigation work, there are several types of professional who do law or law-related work – legal executives, paralegals, licensed conveyancers, notaries, patent attorneys, scriveners even. But the two main types are **solicitors** and **barristers** (I'll get to the rest later).

Solicitors work on their own (a **sole practitioner**) or in **law firms** which are usually **partnerships** (often limited liability partnerships or LLPs, which I'll explain later).

Barristers work in **chambers** (also known as **sets**, a bit like badgers' sets).

Barristers v Solicitors

The basic distinction is that barristers tend to present cases in court (using advocacy skills, which is why they are sometimes called **advocates**) while solicitors tend to do the supporting preparatory work. Lawyers who specialise in disputes work are called **litigators** and legal work involving disputes is called **litigation**. In the old days you needed both a solicitor and a barrister to go to court: you instructed the solicitor who in turn instructed the barrister (by sending the barrister **instructions to counsel** – a **brief** – traditionally bound up with pink ribbon).

But now solicitors are allowed to appear in court (for the top courts they need to have an advocacy qualification called **higher rights of audience**) and barristers are allowed to deal directly with the public.

This change was introduced so that clients don't have to instruct two sets of lawyers (a solicitor and a barrister) when going to court (in France they also have this split between **avocats** and **conseils juridiques** – advocates and legal advisers; but in the US they have a **fused legal profession** where everyone is simply an **attorney** but some specialise in being **trial attorneys**).

However, in practice, in anything other than the most straightforward of cases, you will still need to use both a solicitor and a barrister. This is because there is a lot of work that goes into a case before it gets anywhere near a court. This includes, for instance, collating evidence, compiling statements, serving papers on the other side, negotiating to achieve a settlement and so on. All of this is best done by solicitors.

The barrister will be used at the outset (through what are called **conferences with counsel**, known as 'cons with counsel' – 'counsel' is what solicitors call barristers) to help determine what the strategy should be and to advise on any tricky points of law (barristers do a lot of this advisory work since they act as expert lawyers to whom more generalist solicitors can go). But barristers come into their own when presenting cases and thinking on their feet in court.

Barristers are able to play this role because they are in and out of court all the time. They know what judges are thinking, how they are leaning and how the law is developing. Most judges start out as barristers (although increasingly solicitors are becoming judges too).

This may make the **Bar** (the collective name for barristers) seem incestuous. But in fact they are all technically self-employed. Partners in solicitors' firms are too, but they are also in partnership with each other which binds them together. By contrast, a chambers is a collection of self-employed barristers who come together to share expenses such as premises, a library and, crucially, the use of a **barristers' clerk** (not to be confused with a **clerk to the court** who helps the judge).

A barristers' clerk is not a lawyer. Traditionally, many of them came from London's East End or Essex and followed their fathers into a particular set. But the clerk is a key figure. He is basically a salesman. His job is to get briefs (instructions) for his barristers from firms of solicitors, to match the brief to the barrister he has available, to negotiate the fee with the solicitor and to make sure the fee is paid. So while it helps to be nicely spoken it's even more important to be a bit of a wheeler-dealer. Clerks earn a percentage of their barristers' brief fees, which is why some of them can earn a lot of money.

Increasingly chambers behave like law firms: although the barristers are self-employed they band together with others doing a similar sort of work: as a set gets a reputation in a certain field, it will attract more work from all around in that field, to the benefit of all the barristers in that set. The most prestigious sets have been around for years and it is hard to join them. They recruit the top legal talent.

To be a barrister, you complete your studies and then get **called to the Bar** which is the formal term for meaning that you are admitted (technically qualified) as a barrister. But you can't yet practise (work for clients) as a barrister. First, young barristers have to join a set where they do their **pupillage** (working for a qualified barrister who is called the **pupil master**). And even after that it can still be incredibly difficult to get a **tenancy** (a full-time place in a set, without which you cannot practise). Those that do have their name on the door. I mean this quite literally: walk around any of the four Inns of Court in London which is where barristers work (Gray's Inn, Lincoln's Inn, Middle Temple and Inner Temple – all of which are within a short distance of each other, clustered round the Royal Courts of Justice in the Strand) and you will see office doors with names painted on them.

At the top of the list are QCs (**QC** stands for **Queen's Counsel** and when a king is on the throne they are called KCs, short for King's Counsel). A QC is a senior barrister and you become a QC by being appointed (traditionally by a government minister, now by a panel of senior lawyers). This is called **taking silk** (because QCs traditionally wear silk gowns in court). Barristers who haven't taken silk are called **juniors**. But some barristers never take silk and remain juniors all their lives. This is because becoming a QC is a risk. QCs charge more and, crucially, always work with a junior. This makes them very expensive and means that QCs are only used on big cases. So a barrister has to be confident that they have sufficient of a following amongst solicitors to attract big cases before they take the leap. Rumpole of the Bailey, John Mortimer's famous legal creation, was a criminal barrister who only ever defended people charged with crimes. He never took silk so remained a 'junior' even into his seventies.

In the past it was incredibly hard to start a new chambers. Now it is easier and you will often find that new sets set up physically outside the traditional Inns of Court for the very good reason that they can't find office space there. Although the Inns of Court in London are the national focus for barristers, there are barristers' sets wherever you find courts so the major cities like Manchester and Birmingham have their own sets too.

You may think that being a barrister is better than being a solicitor when it comes to litigation. Certainly it's more glamorous, being on your feet and arguing in court. But being a solicitor is just as satisfying too. In my experience solicitors who specialise in litigation aren't like other lawyers. They tend to know more law for a start (in my experience only tax lawyers know more law than litigators) because they have to apply the law to analyse the legal issues of a case.

If you are a litigator, you have to be able to analyse a set of facts, understand the applicable law and say whether or not there is a case and, if so, the chances of success. You have to be good at spotting the strengths and weaknesses of cases and to be good at driving a hard bargain with the other side. There's a lot of procedure and point-scoring behind the scenes which can win or lose cases. Some of the biggest cases are between the world's largest businesses, with hundreds of millions of pounds at stake, involving a large number of different parties and with a degree of complexity which means they can last for years and years. And it's the solicitor who knows the case far better and for longer than anyone. Litigators love getting their teeth stuck into these sorts of cases.

Criminal Lawyers

So far I've been talking about civil law litigators. I want to end this chapter by going back to where we started: criminal law; and in particular lawyers who do criminal work, in court defending people charged with crimes.

Lawyers who do criminal work are a breed apart. They are often incredibly committed, idealistic people, with a strong sense of justice and right and wrong. This is because they do not earn much.

When you think about it, almost all criminals tend to be poor (consider for a moment that a great deal of crime is caused by drugs: people robbing, stealing and mugging to fund their next hit). So they cannot afford a lawyer. But to ensure that they are properly defended the state pays for their legal representation through **legal aid**. Someone who is eligible for legal aid (it is means tested, meaning that your income and assets are taken into account in calculating whether you are eligible) doesn't have to pay to get legal advice. Instead the lawyer is paid for by the government.

The bulk of legal aid is spent on criminal cases (to ensure everyone gets a fair hearing by having their side presented professionally) as well as some civil cases involving **human rights**, **immigration** and **housing**.

In fact legal aid is like the NHS: it expands to meet demand. So successive governments have tried to rein it in by imposing a series of constraints on legal aid firms. First, they had to fulfil various quality standards ('quality' here meaning the use of processes to ensure similar work is done in the same way to ensure efficiency).

Then the government granted contracts: for any given location a firm would get a legal aid contract to do a certain type of work at a certain rate. However, in some parts of the country for some types of work no firm came forward, leading to legal aid 'deserts'. Then the government imposed caps on what it's prepared to pay and restricted what legal aid is available for.

Fair enough, you might think: why should there be a limitless bucket. But it does mean that someone somewhere is not getting the advice – or the quality of advice – they need and should be entitled to in any wealthy western liberal democracy.

CAB

The other source of social law advice is the **Citizens Advice Bureau** which offers free advice to walk-in customers, mainly on money and legal issues. Often the case workers may not be lawyers as such but have so much practical experience in the particular field that it doesn't actually matter. In any case they will refer issues that turn into cases to local legal aid firms to take forward.

Final Point

Now, and this may surprise you, most lawyers aren't litigators. They don't do court-related work or resolve disputes. What they do is put agreements together, and the bulk of these are based on the law of contract, which is what we are going to look at next.

CHAPTER 4

CONTRACT

Contract – nexus – intention – certain – invitation to treat – offer – acceptance – exclusion clause – incorporation – battle of the forms – terms and conditions (Ts&Cs) – representations – warranties – express – implied – course of dealing – boilerplate – schedules – performance – quantum meruit – frustration – mistake – waiver – force majeure – act of god – term of art – discharged – terminated – remedies – damages – mitigate – consequential loss – rescission – restitution – specific performance – consideration – past consideration – agreement to agree – bargain – deed – capacity – retention of title – assignment – novation – chose in action – Carbolic Smoke Ball Company – commercial law – agency – distribution – joint ventures – supply agreements – banking – construction – employment – contract of service – contract for services – trade union law – media – music – sports – intellectual property – technology – outsourcing – telecoms – shipping – insurance – reinsurance

Cast your mind back to tort. In Chapter 2 I talked about the fact that in the absence of a contract, C (claimant) had to sue in tort. So the snail-in-the-bottle case (*Donoghue v Stevenson*) was about C suing the manufacturer in tort because there wasn't a contract between them. Tort is a wrong committed by someone to someone else. **Contract** is about an agreement between two (or more) people.

So a fundamental difference is that in one (contract) there is a connection (called a contractual **nexus**) between the parties. In the other (tort) they may not even know each other (the way we didn't know each other when I dropped my hammer on you).

Similarly, the point of damages (what the successful claimant is awarded in court) in tort is to put you in the position you were in (or would have been in) before the tort occurred (as if it had *never* happened). In contract the purpose of damages is to put you in the position you would have been if the contract had been properly performed, that is, if it *had* actually happened. One (tort) is a reversion to the status quo ante (the way things were before). The other (contract) is a shift in time forward to the way you expected things to turn out. Get those things clear and I promise you won't get confused (and a promise is really what a contract is).

Contract law is actually the basis for much of our everyday life which is sustained by a network of contracts. You're able to turn on the light because you have a contract with the utility company. When you buy food in the supermarket, there's a contract which you enter into at the check-out (remember the knife-in-the-shop-window case in the Introduction?). When you go to work, you do so pursuant to an employment contract with your employer. When you go on holiday you enter into a contract with the holiday company. When you get on a bus, and so on.

So contracts occur in all sorts of everyday situations as well as between businesses, hence their complexity. Most of the law about contracts has developed from situations in which they go wrong. Two parties will enter into a contract with each other because each thinks he will gain a benefit from doing so. But the bulk of cases arise where one party doesn't, or doesn't get quite the deal he expected (or doesn't like the fact that the other side did a whole lot better out of the deal) or finds that performing his side of the agreement is too onerous or expensive. Instead he will try to wriggle out and call the whole thing off.

For example, a party may raise any one or more of the following issues:

- Is there a contract? I say there's an agreement between us, you say there isn't
- Is a specific term part of it? I say it requires you to do this, you say it doesn't
- Has it been properly performed? I say I've done my bit, you say I haven't
- Has it ended? I say it's over, you say it's still going

- Has liability (for poor- or non-performance) been excluded? I say you didn't do your bit properly, you say you didn't have to

And so on. These are just examples. In general the courts lean towards upholding contracts, otherwise life would grind to a halt if people could change their minds whenever they liked. So over the centuries contract law has developed through cases in which contracts were upheld or not for specific reasons, or in which they were modified. And over that time various principles of contract law have emerged. For instance, one that house buyers come across is *caveat emptor* which means 'buyer beware'. It means it's up to you to satisfy yourself that the house is OK and the seller owns it.

1.   Is There A Contract?

So what does the law require there to be in order for two parties to have a binding agreement between them?

Well, evidently it doesn't have to be in writing, which may come as something of a surprise. I said 'evidently' on purpose because in some cases it does (the writing is evidence of the contract's existence), most importantly when it involves land because land has always been a serious item of property and a store of value that lasts forever (see Chapter 6).

But in the main contracts don't have to be in writing. It helps if they are because then you know what the terms are and if the piece of paper is signed it indicates an intention on the part of the signatory to enter into an agreement. But this isn't necessary, just as in the old days when people used bits of paper called cheques to pay each other, a cheque didn't have to be a bit of paper with a bank's logo on it but could in theory have been written on the side of a cow (I'm not sure if this actually happened or whether a maverick judge just gave it as a legally possible example).

Now, before you start worrying that you can find yourself in a contract without ever intending to be, one of the requirements is **intention**: each of the parties must have intended to enter into contractual relations with the other.

Nor can the contract be vague. It has to be, in legal terms, **certain**. That is, key aspects (such as price) must be clear.

So how, then, does a contract come about at all?

This may seem a bit weird but basically it happens when one party makes an offer which the other party accepts. What throws a lot of law students is how much case law there is on this part of contract law, especially when it's the first big bit of the subject that they encounter. But it's relevant for two reasons: for deciding whether there is a contract at all; and for determining the point at which the contract came into existence and, therefore, what is in the contract and what falls outside it. I'll explain.

Remember that in the Introduction I mentioned that a shopkeeper put a flick-knife in the window of his shop and someone came in to buy it? Displaying a flick-knife (one where the blade springs out from the handle) for sale like that was actually a criminal offence at the time (it probably still is) and the shopkeeper was prosecuted. Although this was a criminal case (see Chapter 1), contract law became relevant.

The shopkeeper argued that he wasn't offering the knife for sale: it was up to the prospective customer to enter the shop and to offer to buy the knife from him at the price displayed; it was then up to the shopkeeper to decide whether or not to accept the offer and so sell the knife (for instance, in all likelihood the shopkeeper wouldn't have sold it to a child or an obvious villain). The court agreed. So the shopkeeper got off because the offence hadn't been properly framed. The court said that putting the knife in the window was an **invitation to treat** (that is an invitation to open a negotiation that might lead to a contract), not an offer of a contract (an offer for sale) itself. So the shopkeeper wasn't offering the knife for sale. Putting it in the window was merely an invitation to treat. On such small distinctions do big things turn.

So there is no contract until there has been both an **offer** and **acceptance**. Now, the point at which an offer is accepted is the point at which the contract comes into being and from then on the terms are fixed. So the actual point at which a contract is concluded can be as crucial as whether there is a contract at all. This means – which can be hard to grasp – that if I make an offer and you make a counter-offer to my offer, your counter-offer discharges my offer: if I reject your counter-offer you can't take me up on my original offer because it's been superseded.

One of the things that confuses students is how many cases about offer and acceptance turn on when letters were posted, which now seems very old-technology. Before the postal service, agreements were made face to face. So it was easy to establish whether and when a contract came into existence. But as soon as snail-mail started (as novel in its day as the internet was in mine) it gave rise to all sorts of issues, because people started making and accepting offers by post. The main issue was: what happened if one of the two parties changed their mind before the letter arrived? What happened if an acceptance got lost in the post?

What the courts decided was that as soon as an offeree (someone who's received an offer) posts a letter of acceptance, the act of posting the acceptance means the offer has been accepted (even before it actually arrives). The reason why this is a big deal (apart from the obvious one that it determines that a contract now subsists) is that, once an offer has been accepted, the terms of the contract are final. Neither party can add an extra term or modify the existing ones. So what?

So a lot. Read on.

2.   What Are The Terms? (The Importance Of Exclusion Clauses)

Thornton v Shoe Lane Parking was a case about a car park off Fleet Street. The claimant had parked his car. The car had been damaged. So he sued the car park owner. The car park owner said: 'Aha, we are covered by the comprehensive exclusion clause printed on the back of the parking ticket which you took from the machine just before the barrier lifted and you drove in. So therefore we are not liable to you.'

The judge disagreed. He said that the contract had been concluded before the machine printed the receipt. So it was no good sticking an exclusion clause on the back of the receipt because by then the contract (and all its terms) had come into existence. Presumably the analysis was something like: the driver offered to park there for the advertised price; which the machine accepted by taking his money; the ticket was therefore issued (as evidence of the contract) *after* the contract had come into existence, even if only a *scintilla temporis* (Latin expression beloved of lawyers meaning an 'instant of time') later.

Since the **exclusion clause** printed on the back of the ticket came too late to be part of the contract, the car park was liable for the damage. I expect the very next day they put their exclusion clause on a board just as you drive in and before you take the ticket. By the way, guess who the judge was? Yup, Denning.

Of course, contracts nowadays contain extensive exclusion clauses to the extent that you wonder whether there is any obligation to do anything at all. But even if these exclusion clauses have been properly incorporated, recent consumer legislation has watered down much of the effect of many of these clauses.

In particular the Unfair Contract Terms Act 1977 (pronounced 'Ucta' by lawyers) said that you can never exclude liability for injury or death and in all other cases any attempted exclusion has to be 'reasonable'. In addition the Sale of Goods Act 1979 lays down rules (about the quality and suitability of goods sold in a contract) which cannot be shirked.

Thornton v Shoe Lane Parking was a case about **incorporation**. Not in the sense of incorporating a company (I'll come to that later) but whether the exclusion clause was incorporated into the contract. Denning said it wasn't.

Offer and acceptance lead to what is sometimes called the **battle of the forms**: it's normal for businesses to have standard **terms and conditions** (meaning the clauses that make up the contract, also known as **Ts&Cs**) printed on the back of their stationery. So when two businesses enter into an agreement with each other, and each writes to the other confirming, whose standard terms apply? It depends on who accepted whose offer and whether the terms were explicitly referred to. It can be like ping-pong, backwards and forwards. The last to be incorporated before the agreement is reached wins, superseding whatever might have been tabled earlier. Hence the expression 'battle of the forms'.

The clauses in a contract may themselves vary in importance. Some are called 'conditions' and others 'terms' depending on whether they go to the root of the contract (conditions) and allow termination for breach, or vary in importance (terms) where termination for breach depends on the impact of that breach. There is a further distinction between **representations** (known as 'reps') and **warranties**. Some parts of a contract may be **express** (they are actually set out in the contract). Others may be **implied** (they aren't set out anywhere but without them the contract wouldn't work so they are deemed to have been meant by the parties to be included) often through a **course of dealing** – two parties trading with each other regularly.

There is a lot of gubbins in a legal agreement: clauses that are pretty standard in all contracts, such as provisions saying how parties serve notice on each other (deliver important information to each other – for instance if one is late in doing his bit and the other needs to notify him formally that he is) or saying which law applies (in the UK, usually English law) or which courts should hear any dispute. All of this is known as **boilerplate**. It needs to be correct but isn't where the heart of the agreement is to be found. Often that's in appendices or **schedules** to the contract (especially if it is a relatively standard type of agreement) where the subject-matter and price are often detailed.

3.   Has It Been Properly Performed?

Okay, so we've reached the point where there is a contract and we know its terms.

Both parties may accept this but one may claim that the other has failed to perform its side of the deal. The question then is: what constitutes good **performance**?

In terms of performance, the courts say that you have to do exactly what you say you will. Part-performance is generally not enough to get part-payment unless the contract is one based on **quantum meruit** (you get paid for the worth of what you've done even if you haven't finished – many building contracts are like this). But there are exceptions.

On the whole the courts are loath to let people wriggle out of their contractual obligations. Some of the extenuating circumstances that parties may plead include **frustration** (that a subsequent change in circumstances makes it impossible to perform or commercially pointless to do so), **mistake** (one or other entered into the contract under a misapprehension), **waiver** (that one side didn't perform but the other side waived its right to require performance – for instance by doing nothing for a long time in response). The one that non-lawyers mention the most is **force majeure** (aka **act of god**) meaning that performance was made impossible – for instance through war, terrorist outrage, violent weather, etc, etc. Funnily enough the term 'force majeure' is not a **term of art**, in other words it is not a term to which the law ascribes any specific, technical legal meaning. Unless the parties specifically include it in the contract and define what they mean by it, a party cannot raise it later.

On the whole the courts have kept these excuses within narrow confines – again because otherwise life would become less certain if it was easy to ignore a contractual commitment. In fact contracts were regarded as absolute commitments (parties had to include in the contract the reasons for which non-performance would be excusable) until *Taylor v Caldwell* (1863) in which the fact that a music hall had actually burnt down was treated, sensibly enough, as a valid reason for not honouring a booking.

4. Has It Ended?

One party may claim that the contract has ended so (further) performance is not required. Contract law uses the term **discharged**: has the contract been discharged? This can occur because it has been performed (both sides have done their bit), because it has been **terminated** (by mutual agreement), because it has been broken (breach of contract – see below) or because it has been frustrated (see above).

Remedies For Breach Of Contract

Assuming one party can claim that the other is in the wrong for non, or only partial, performance, the next question is: what **remedies** are open to C?

Whereas in tort the purpose of **damages** (monetary compensation) is to put C in the position she would have been in before or without the tortious act occurring, the purpose of damages in contract is to put C in the same position as if the contract *had been properly performed*. So in tort it took a long time for the courts to be prepared to award damages for loss of profit; whereas in contract what C wants is precisely the profit or gain that C would otherwise have obtained if the contract had been properly performed.

So how are damages calculated? Damages should make good any harm or loss caused to C or C's property (for example a reduction in the value of her property due to the breach of contract). The party in breach has to pay damages for losses past and future but there must be a genuine estimate of future loss (that rule against penalties again). And C must have done her best to **mitigate** her loss (reduce it as much as possible); for example, a wronged employee must try to find another job rather than just claiming his old salary from his former employer. If he hasn't, the court will deduct a sum from the damages to make up for the amount he could be earning.

There are other limits. As in tort there is a test for remoteness of damage, although the test is a bit different. The rule was established in *Hadley v Baxendale* (1854) and says that damages should cover **consequential loss** – what would be seen as naturally arising from the breach or what could be supposed to have been in the contemplation of the parties when the contract was made.

Speaking of tort, and just to confuse you further, you can get tortious liability in contract if the contract has been negligently performed – but for our purposes we don't need to go there.

Apart from damages C can get a whole lot of other contractual remedies such as: **rescission** (tear the contract up); **restitution** (put C back where she was); and **specific performance** (get the contract performed as C wanted). In employment contracts you only get damages: an employee won't be required to go back to an employer with whom they have fallen out.

The Language Of Contract

Consideration – a contract is a mutual exchange: one party provides a service; the other party pays for it. If only one party is providing anything, there's a risk there isn't a contract at all. This is because the contract lacks what is known as consideration. It's for this reason that you may see a contract say something strange such as: 'In consideration of the payment of £1, receipt of which is hereby acknowledged'. In practice the £1 never changes hands, but this explicit reference to consideration prevents the lack of it from being a reason for saying there isn't a contract at all. There's another saying: **past consideration** is no consideration which simply means that something done in the past isn't sufficient to sustain a contract entered into now.

An **agreement to agree** – is itself not binding and is not a contract (at least in the UK; it can be elsewhere).

A **bargain** – is another legal term for 'agreement' or 'contract'. It's not something you buy in a sale.

A **deed** – is simply an agreement the signing of which has been witnessed (which means that evidentially it can be stronger and no consideration is required).

Capacity – is the ability of a party to enter into a contract. Children, for instance, lack capacity.

Retention of title (aka *Romalpa* clause) – is a way of ensuring that when a manufacturer sells to a distributor, the manufacturer can get its goods back from the purchaser if the distributor fails to pay it (named after the case that gave rise to it).

Assignment – transferring a contract to another party.

Novation – another way of transferring a contract, but by extinguishing it and replacing it with an identical one with another party.

Chose in action – the bundle of rights that arise under a contract and which can be assigned (transferred) to someone else in order to bring a claim ('chose' from the French for 'thing' and pronounced like 'shows').

Invitation To The Ball

Law students at uni hold black-tie all-nighters called Carbolic Smoke Balls. They're balls (parties) named after a famous contract case (another example, I'm afraid, of legal humour) involving the **Carbolic Smoke Ball Company**.

The Carbolic Smoke Ball Company made and marketed a thing called (you guessed it) the Carbolic Smoke Ball. Basically it was advertised as a cure for flu. The company said that anyone who tried it and was dissatisfied could get their money back. When the Carbolic Smoke Ball Company was sued by disgruntled consumers it argued that the offer was mere advertising puff ('puff' is a legal term meaning something too ephemeral to have legal consequence) and not meant to be a binding commitment – how could it be when it was broadcast to the world.

The court disagreed. The Carbolic Smoke Ball Company lost the case and presumably went bust but lives on whenever law students party.

Contract In Practice

Now you know about contract law, I can begin to introduce you to a wide range of legal specialisations that emanate from it.

The first is loosely **commercial law**, that's to say, contracts as used in business. This covers all sorts of different types of commercial contracts including **agency**, **distribution** and **joint ventures**. The reason why agency and distribution are singled out is because a lot of commercial contracts are about manufacturers getting agents and distributors to sell their products – agents do so on the manufacturer's behalf for a commission; distributors buy the goods off the manufacturer and keep whatever profit they make from the on-sale. **Supply agreements** (where a supplier supplies something – say a farmer supplying produce to a supermarket) are also commercial agreements. A joint venture is when two commercial parties decide to run a business venture together. All of these are based on the law of contract, but agency is an established and complex sub-branch of contract in its own right.

Banking is a huge area of law but in essence a loan agreement is just that, a contract to lend money in return for interest and repayment of the amount lent. It is the basis of much of the work done by law firms in the City of London, as we shall see.

Construction and engineering law is just another form of contract law, mentioned in the last chapter because it gives rise to such a lot of disputes.

Employment law is also based on contract. A **contract of service** is an employment contract whereas a **contract for services** is a consultancy agreement where the consultant remains self-employed. However, there is now a huge amount of regulation grafted on to employment contracts to ensure that employees aren't exploited, sacked or made redundant unfairly, do have parental rights, can work flexibly and aren't disadvantaged by disability. One area of law I want to mention here is **trade union law**. It's based partly on contract, mainly on employment and the rights of workers, and also on human rights. A couple of law firms have become well known for specialising in it.

Media law is a relatively recent specialisation and is an umbrella term for a number of different strands, again based on contract, such as the publishing (hard copy and electronic) of books, magazines and newspapers; broadcasting (television, radio); multimedia (including video games and DVD); and the exploitation of the associated commercial rights. Sub-specialisations within it include **music** and **sports** law (acting respectively for musicians, their managers and record companies; and for athletes, sportsmen, their agents and the media that exploit the commercial rights). Also relevant is **intellectual property** law (rights of ownership in creative arts and industrial innovation) which I'll explore later. A lot of media law is about exploiting intellectual property (IP) rights, such as image rights. Media lawyers also tend to cover the tort of defamation (see Chapter 2).

Technology law started off as the law relating to computing – essentially a form of commercial law involving the buying and selling of technology. But it soon developed into the law relating to data – for instance, when is an electronic signature valid – and now includes data protection legislation. A lot of big outsourcing deals (where a business gets someone else to run part of its operations) are essentially about outsourcing a business's technology requirements to a specialist provider. So although **outsourcing** is about more general, commercial transactions that don't have to involve technology at all, a lot of technology lawyers have moved into this area.

Telecoms wasn't an area of practice prior to the privatisation of British Telecom in 1984. That created a new telecommunications industry with a brand new regulatory infrastructure in which lawyers started to specialise.

With platforms (TV, DVDs, devices, downloads, streaming) and content (films, music, video games, news) converging, telecoms, technology and media law have started to overlap and converge. All three are underpinned by IP.

Shipping was mentioned in the last chapter. It's based on contract law but has its own terminology. There's more on shipping in Chapter 8.

Two areas related to shipping, also based on contract, are **insurance** and **reinsurance** (the two are distinct specialisations though linked) which are about the taking on of insured risk in return for a premium. Each is an industry in its own right. As with banking law they have developed their own terminology and you can't practise in the field without understanding both the jargon and how the industry works. We'll look at these in Chapter 8 too.

It All Connects

Now that we've done contract and tort you can see that one way of looking at tort is to say that it's where the law provides a remedy even in the absence of a contractual connection between the parties. And by 'provides a remedy' I mean: allows C to pursue a claim against D – which is what litigation (covered in the last chapter) is about. It all connects.

So far we've covered three of what I consider to be the five pillars of English law. We've done criminal, tort and contract. Now you need to strap your seat belt on for the fourth: equity.

CHAPTER 5

JUDGES BREAKING LAW: EQUITY

Trust – legal title – delivery – legal owner – on trust – trustee – equitable owner – beneficiary – beneficial owner – rule against perpetuities – void ab initio – settle – trust for sale – joint tenants – tenants in common – jointly – in common – clog on the equity of redemption – bare trust – secret trust – will – probate – testamentary disposition – codicil – ambulatory – testator – testatrix – intestate – bona vacantia – hotchpot – promissory estoppel – dirty hands – charities – education – tax

I'm sorry to have to do this to you. Just when things seemed to be going so well we're going to take a sharp turn to the left and cover equity – which throws a real spanner in the works. Equity is bizarre. So put your seat belt on. This is where our nice and orderly exposition of the law suddenly lurches off course and plunges into the unknown.

Because equity is what judges keep under the bench and pull out when they want to break the law.

It's what Denning used in order to arrive at a just outcome notwithstanding what the law actually said. So in this respect judges are law breakers: they break the law by substituting equity.

If you find this weird, join the club.

Equity

Back in the middle ages there were different courts of law. There were manorial courts set up by local lords which applied local customary law. There were ecclesiastical (church) courts. Then there were the courts of common law (hearing cases between subjects, hence 'common', rather than cases in which the king was involved).

These courts applied and developed the basic common law principles of tort, contract, property and something called restitution (giving back or making good – nowadays equivalent to damages, more or less). But as common law became established, judges wouldn't depart from it. They followed precedent (previous similar cases) rigidly.

However, this often led to manifest injustice. So, for example, if someone who owed money (a debtor) paid off the debt and forgot or failed to have the bond (piece of paper recording the debt) cancelled, the creditor could still seek payment from the debtor, even though he had already been paid back once.

In cases of injustice like this, the debtor would petition the king's chancellor – the king's most important minister – to redress this wrong by saying the wrong was 'inequitable' (unfair). The chancellor received these types of petitions ('bills of complaint') from courts all over and the chancellor's court (which became known as the court of chancery) used 'equity' to right these wrongs.

This led to two types of court: the King's (or Queen's) Bench; and Chancery. Chancery was the more intellectual of the two. Knock-about cases that were tried on their facts went to KB. Cases involving much paperwork and the construing of documents and deeds ended up in Chancery; cases involving wills, for example. This meant that two systems of law existed in parallel, common law and equity.

And this persisted until as recently as the Judicature Act 1873, which decreed that there was one system of courts but they should apply both sets of law (I'm being a bit misleading to call equity a set of laws: the chancellor's decisions weren't recorded in the sense of establishing precedents as the common law does – one reason why Chancery could depart from precedent). The Judicature Act came in a good twenty years after Charles Dickens published *Bleak House*, his satire on the protracted process of the Chancery court.

Trusts

OK. So we've established how equity arose. But what about trusts? Where do they fit?

A **trust** is both beautifully simple and unbelievably complex. Let's say I've got some money that I want to give to my son Frankie. He's not around at the moment and I need to go. But he'll be around later. So I give the money to you (because I trust you) for you to give to him in my absence when he turns up.

I have created a trust.

You hold the cash. On the face of it, it's your money. You have **legal title** to it (as with many types of property, legal title to money passes with **delivery**, that's to say when I give it to you). So you could spend it if you liked. You could go into a shop and the shopkeeper (the one with the knife in the window) could accept the money from you because he'd be legally entitled to assume it was yours (you might get a bottle of ginger beer plus snail in return). You are therefore the **legal owner** of the money.

But you and I know it's not really your money. You are holding it temporarily **on trust** for Frankie. You are merely the **trustee** of the money. In equity, Frankie is the real owner. He's not the legal owner. At law, you are – you have title to it. But he is the **equitable owner**. He owns the economic benefit of the money. He is the one due to benefit from the money. He is the **beneficiary** of the trust and is the **beneficial owner** of the money (beneficial and equitable mean the same here). And it's so simple it doesn't even need to be in writing.

But here comes the complexity. Frankie takes five years to turn up. In the meantime I kick the bucket. What are you supposed to do with the money in the meantime? Invest it? In what? Who keeps any profit? Can you deduct your expenses? Supposing I didn't give you the money but in my will I said that Frankie should get it when he was old enough. Supposing I then have several other children. Are they included? What order do they get it in? How do the trustees know who all the eligible children are? And so on and so on.

In fact trusts became so complicated that they threatened to tie up property (principally land) forever. So the **rule against perpetuities** grew up in common law, making a trust invalid if there could be any possibility it might last for more than 21 years after the death of a particular person already living at the time it was set up. The test was incredibly complex and the result was that the entire trust could be **void ab initio** (without legal effect from the outset).

So, after a few hundred years, the Perpetuities and Accumulations Act 1964 was passed to try to improve things. It said trusts could include a set maximum period of 80 years or that trustees could simply 'wait and see' whether a trust did in fact outlast the maximum perpetuity rule period (I say this hesitantly as you'd need a perpetuity to grasp the rule against perpetuities). Good news, though: the whole thing has now been replaced by a straightforward maximum period of 125 years, under the Perpetuities and Accumulations Act 2009.

All sorts of case law and legislation popped up to deal with these issues. Things with titles like the Settled Land Act (to **settle** is to put property on trust; the one who does it is the 'settlor'); the Trustee Act; the Trustee Investment Act. Of course a lot of these trusts were created to pass property on to the next generation, which is where wills, probate and trusts started to come together. In fact in one year (1925 – a vintage year for legislation as we'll see in the next chapter) the Settled Land Act 1925 (how you settle land on trust), the Trustee Act 1925 (how trust property is looked after) and the Administration of Estates Act 1925 (how trust property passes when the owner has died) were introduced.

But they were by no means the first.

Way back in 1536, Henry VIII had presided over one of the most significant pieces of law-making: the Statute of Uses. A 'use' was the original name for a trust and the beneficiary was originally called the *cestui que use* (a bizarre combination of French, English and possibly Latin, pronounced by lawyers as 'settee key use') which in time became 'cestui que trust'.

Maitland, one of the great scholars of English law, said: 'If we were asked what is the greatest and most distinctive achievement performed by Englishmen in the field of jurisprudence I cannot think that we should have any better answer to give than this, namely the development…of the trust idea.' Which just shows that he needed to get out more. Because other countries like France and Germany (in fact, the whole of Europe) have managed to get by without the trust concept at all, thank you very much.

But being serious for a mo, the trust concept is in truth fantastically flexible. For instance, if you and your partner own the place you live in, the chances are that you own it as trustees. When two people buy a house together they are the legal owners but they hold the beneficial interest in the house on **trust for sale** for themselves as either **joint tenants** or **tenants in common**.

Although the beneficiaries are called tenants this isn't in the sense of tenants who are renting (although you could say they are tenants in the sense that the legal owners are landlords). No, I think it's more like the original Latin (*teneo* = I hold) in that they are holding jointly or in common. **Jointly** means that each owns the whole with the other so when one dies the other automatically gets the whole. **In common** means each owns half so if one dies the other only gets the additional half if left it in the will.

This may sound like a lot of legal waffle but it can be hugely significant in the real world. A husband and wife may own their home as joint tenants, but if one of them becomes bankrupt (for instance from a failed business venture), the other will lose his or her share. If, however, they had severed the joint tenancy and held as tenants in common, each would hang on to his or her own share; so if the business fails, creditors get half the house – the half owned by the one who was in business – but not all of it.

Dancing In Clogs On The Equity Of Redemption

Staying with residential property for a moment, equity is the reason why you can always pay off your mortgage early even if you may be charged a fee for doing so (I was going to say 'penalty' but at law penalties are not enforceable). Equity says that it's unfair to stop anyone paying off a debt if they want to. And any attempt to negate this is called (quaintly) a **clog on the equity of redemption**.

Trusts range from the simple **bare trust** (which doesn't even have to be in writing) to complicated vehicles set up by extensive trust deeds. You can even have a **secret trust** (for instance where the settlor establishes a trust for his mistress and illegitimate kids but doesn't want anyone to know). Trusts are the basis of unit trusts (investment funds), offshore financing vehicles in the world's capital markets, pension funds and charities. They can be created during the settlor's life or by will on his or her death, so enabling the settlor to decide how he wants his property to devolve after his death. He can exert control beyond the grave. This is why wills, trusts and probate are lumped together.

Wills And Probate

A **will** is a document that sets out what you want to happen to your assets when you die. **Probate** is what actually does happen to them. It's how your estate is wound up. Trusts are what people use to transfer their assets to the next generation.

A will is just a bit of paper in which the testator (the person making the will) leaves his estate (his property and possessions) to whoever he wants. That's the case in the UK. In some countries you don't have freedom of **testamentary disposition** as it's called, which means the freedom to dispose of your estate (pass it on to whoever you want). Instead it has to go to your children in equal shares; or it has to go to the maintenance of your family, which on reflection sounds pretty sensible. But in the UK you can give it to whoever you want.

Of course, if you can use a bit of paper (a will) to leave your assets to anyone, the scope for fraud is huge. In 1837, the Wills Act was passed which laid down the principles that still govern the validity of wills today. The WA37 said that a will was only valid if signed by the testator in the presence of two witnesses each of whom had to sign in the testator's presence.

The interesting question is, I think, why Parliament suddenly decided in 1837 that the country needed a piece of legislation on wills. And the answer, I would guess, is that by 1837 there were enough people around with assets to leave to make it worthwhile; at a time when writing was becoming more prevalent; but before technology enabled successive drafts of documents to be kept on computer. In other words the WA37 was designed to prevent fraud.

The cases on wills since 1837 – and there have been a lot – have involved courts trying to find ways to uphold wills where nothing fraudulent went on but the legal niceties were not always followed. So it soon became established that the two witnesses didn't have to sign at the same time; and that the testator didn't have to witness a witness's signature if, later, the witness said the signature on the will was his. Nor did they have to be in the same room as long as there was a sufficient sightline to constitute a single signing.

There was also a lot of case law about successive wills or, rather, testamentary dispositions (leaving property by will) because you can always add to a will at any time before death (through a supplementary document called a **codicil**) or get rid of a will altogether and substitute a new one if you want: a will is said to be **ambulatory** (from the Latin meaning to walk or move, hence 'ambulance') which conveys nicely this sense that a will can be amended or revoked at any point in time before the testator's death (it's kind of strolling along from moment to moment).

Nowadays anyone with substantial wealth will go to a lawyer to draw up their will and law firms keep successive drafts of documents on computer so it is much easier to trace the development of a document and much harder to commit a fraud. So the courts these days bend over backwards to uphold wills. This is because a will is an expression of testamentary intent: it's what the **testator** wants to happen to his (or her – in which case she is a **testatrix**) property. Because if the courts say a will is invalid, the deceased is said to have died intestate (**intestate** means dying without leaving a will) and intestacy is a whole other can of worms, so to speak.

Intestacy is a complex set of rules that determines to whom an estate is distributed in the absence of a valid will. Essentially, the rules ensure that immediate family members take and, in their absence, more distant relatives and so on until people have been found to whom to distribute the estate. If there aren't any, it goes to the crown as **bona vacantia** ('vacant goods' in Latin) which means the government gets to keep it and spend it.

One element of this – called **hotchpot** – was a student nightmare in my day. It basically said that adult children had to bring back into account (that is, have deducted from their equal shares of the pot) amounts they'd already received from the intestate parent while he was alive. Note: hotchpot, not hotchpotch. But now thankfully abolished by the Law Reform (Succession) Act 1995.

Dirty Hands

So that's how equity, trusts, wills and probate fit together. Denning had a field day with equity. One of his earliest memorable cases (in 1947) was called *High Trees*. It's the name of a residential block of flats in Clapham, south London, which still exists and the case concerned rent payable during the 1939-45 war. Basically, Denning said that the landlord (L) had waived the right to receive the rent from the tenant (T). L couldn't claim for it now since the obligation to pay it had arisen in the past (during the war) when L hadn't pursued it. Speaking of the need for 'a new equity', Denning applied the equitable remedy of **promissory estoppel** to achieve fairness. He said that, if L made a promise (not to seek rent) which T relied and acted on, L couldn't in equity go back on his word if it would be to T's detriment to do so.

Fairness also explains another equitable principle, that of **dirty hands**. Someone seeking an equitable remedy can't come before the court 'with dirty hands' which means simply that if you are asking a court to do what is right and fair in the circumstances, you've got to be behaving in a right and fair way yourself.

Trusts-Related Law

Apart from wills, trusts and probate there are other areas involving equity that might not seem so obvious.

For example, **charities** law is about the law governing charitable institutions. The charitable or not-for-profit sector (the 'third sector' as it is known, to distinguish it from the public and private sectors) is huge in the UK. But, quite apart from well-known charities such as the RSPCA and Cancer Research, many organisations are charities in legal structure, including most private schools. Local authorities often need advice on charities law because of land left to them in the past for charitable purposes.

The principal applicable law is the Charities Act 2006 which lays down thirteen charitable purposes. These are important because an asset or a gift that falls within one of them is generally exempt from tax. Whether a purpose is charitable or not may depend on negotiation with the Charity Commissioners, hence the need for legal advice. The reason why charities law is related to trusts law is because charities are in essence trusts with trustees.

Education is a relatively new area of law and, like all new areas of law, is a ragbag that brings together some strands of established law that otherwise exist in isolation from each other. So some of it is charity law (which is what most schools and colleges are); some is regulatory (a succession of Education Acts embodying government policy on education); some is about the rights of the individual to be educated; some is trade union law in relation to teachers; some is the law relating to premises and health & safety (which we'll cover later); some is the law relating to children and social services.

Tax is a fiendishly difficult area of law that is *sui generis* (Latin for 'of its own type'). It is a unique area of law that is self-contained and sits on its own. But it comes up a lot in trusts because much of the motivation to use a trust is to minimise tax, especially as assets are passed between generations.

Tax falls into two distinct areas: personal tax and corporate tax. It is entirely statute-based: the government passes new laws each year following the budget which add to, amend and complicate the existing law – which is why there's a tax committee that spends its time trying to simplify the stuff. But there is important case law determining, for instance, what is tax evasion (bad; a criminal offence) and what is tax avoidance (traditionally acceptable; legal ways of reducing your tax bill).

Everything in law has a tax aspect. No lawyer gives advice on anything without consulting a tax colleague, because they know more law than anyone else. In essence, government tries to levy a tax every time money changes hands. When tax rates on income and capital gains are different, analysing whether (and ensuring) a transaction involves one rather than the other can be key.

Final point: you might think that tax lawyers compete with accountants who do tax. In a sense they do. But, by and large, lawyers advise on the law (whether or not there is a liability to tax) while accountants focus on the figures (though they are familiar with the law too). The bigger the amount at stake the more likely you are to involve both a tax lawyer and an accountant.

Now, the most common type of property that is subject to trusts is 'real property' (land) – which is what we'll look at next.

CHAPTER 6

REAL ESTATE

Property law – land law – real property – property in rem – chattels – property in personam – freehold – leasehold – lessor – lessee – premium – reversioner – ground rent – service charge – covenants – quiet enjoyment – right of entry – forfeit the lease – negative covenants – successors in title – positive covenant – common parts – flying freehold – leasehold enfranchisement – permitted use – tenant's covenant – assign – licence to assign – unreasonably withheld – upwards only – voids – anchor tenant – rent-free period – turnover rent – dilapidations – lease – tenancy – surrender – rights of occupation – evict – statutory tenancies – land registration – conveyances – easement – first registration – registered land – transfer – investigation of title – defects in title – vacant possession – sitting tenant – consideration – licensed conveyancers – trespass to land – nuisance – occupiers' liability – *Rylands v Fletcher* – residential conveyancing – commercial property – planning – planning permission – construction – property finance – mortgagee – mortgagor – landlord & tenant (L&T) – housing – welfare – environment – REIT (real estate investment trust) – caveat emptor – adverse possession – affidavit

The one pillar of law we haven't covered so far is **property law** or **land law** as it used to be called (the smart name for property now is real estate). It's often referred to by lawyers as **real property** (**property in rem**, that is land or attached to the land) as against **chattels** which are movable goods (**property in personam** or personal property). There are two forms of legal title to property: freehold and leasehold.

Freehold v Leasehold

Freehold means you own the land for ever. **Leasehold** is a lesser title which is carved out of a freehold and is for a term of years. These leases can be for any length of time but traditionally they are for terms of 99, 125 or 999 years. In other words they will outlive the **lessor** (the freeholder who grants the lease) and the **lessee** (to whom the lease is granted). This means that to all intents and purposes a long lease is almost the same as owning the freehold. The lessee can sell the lease to someone else if he wants. In fact, he probably bought it with a mortgage and the **premium** (the purchase price he has paid to the lessor) will be quite substantial: a flat on a long lease in central London can be worth hundreds of thousands of pounds.

Now, when the 99 years are up, the leasehold will merge back into the freehold, which is why the lessor is also called the **reversioner** because the flat will revert back to him.

There is usually annual **ground rent** to pay but this is often just a few hundred pounds paid once a year. There is also a **service charge** to pay for the upkeep of the building (including insurance) in which the flat is located because the lessee as owner of the flat is responsible for paying his share of the building's maintenance. A well-maintained building will contribute to the value of the flat or at least to the ease with which it can be sold.

You may have noticed that I've been mentioning flats quite a lot in connection with leasehold. That's because almost all flats are leasehold. In fact a common question is: why are flats leasehold and isn't a freehold flat better because it lasts for ever?

Short answer: no.

Covenants: Positive And Negative

If you look at a lease you will see that it contains loads of clauses called **covenants**. A covenant is just the legal term for a promise. The lessee covenants to pay the rent and service charge, to decorate the flat from time to time, not to make a noise, not to keep pets, not to run a business, not to use it for immoral purposes, etc, etc. In return the lessor gives a covenant of **quiet enjoyment**: if the lessee keeps his side of the deal, the lessor will leave him alone. The lessor also covenants to keep the building in good repair (that's what the service charge is for) and properly insured (ditto), both of which the lessor will charge back to the building's lessees. If the lessee fails to keep his covenants, the lessor has a **right of entry** and can go to court to **forfeit the lease** (take it back).

Now, there's a rule in land law that only **negative covenants** run with the land. And this is the key to why you don't want a freehold flat.

What on earth does this mean? It means that only promises *not* to do something attach to the land itself and therefore bind subsequent purchasers (called **successors in title**).

Let me give you a simple freehold example. A landowner sells off a portion of his land. The bit he keeps we'll call A. The bit he sells we'll call B. He imposes on the buyer of B two covenants. One is to put up a fence between the two properties. The other is not to run a business on land B (because the landowner doesn't want to be disturbed). When the person who bought B sells it on, only the second covenant (not to run a business) will bind the buyer. The first (to maintain a fence) won't. That's because maintaining a fence is a **positive covenant**. It requires you to do something rather than merely refrain from doing something. And land law says that a covenant which requires you to actually do something (rather than just refrain from doing something) cannot bind successors in title unless it is put in a contract to which they are a party.

Right Of Support

Now, let's go back to the flat. Let's say it's a first floor flat and there's a flat on the ground floor. In theory the ground floor lessee could knock his flat down. A covenant to provide support to the flat on the first floor is a positive covenant and does not run with the land. Leasehold avoids this, because the lessor stipulates in his lease with each lessee that they must support each others' flats. It also helps that there is a lessor because he can hold the **common parts** (the bits of the building used communally, such as the staircase and a common water tank if there is one, plus the common plumbing and wiring to outside) for the benefit of all the lessees.

That's why if you do by chance buy a freehold flat on the first floor it's known as a **flying freehold**. People who do often end up suing their solicitor (professional indemnity – see earlier). It's also why lawyers laugh if estate agents say enthusiastically that a flat is freehold rather than leasehold. Sounds good. But it ain't.

Two other problems with leasehold flats: the lease runs out; and the service charge can get out of hand.

Short Leases And Leasehold Enfranchisement

Once a lease gets down to anything less than about 25 years it becomes difficult to sell. That's because people won't buy it because they are thinking of the person who will buy from the person who will buy from them. Most people need a mortgage to buy the place they live in. Mortgages tend to be for around 20-25 years – the period over which the loan to buy the flat is repaid. Mortgage lenders won't look at short-term leases for this reason.

Faced with thousands of flats becoming worthless in big city centres, successive governments have put in place legislation called **leasehold enfranchisement**. This means transferring the freehold of a building to all the lessees in it. When you think about it, the reversion on a building that is fully let on long leases isn't worth much: at best it's the freeholder's great-grandchildren who may be around to get the flats back. So this legislation puts in place a mechanism to pay the freeholder the current value of the reversion (which the lessees club together to do). Then they can grant themselves extensions whenever they like.

Service Charge And Management Companies

This also tackles the second issue: lessors using service charges in unscrupulous ways to make money out of lessees (for instance, getting 'repairs' done by their own workmen at inflated prices). There is legislation in place to ensure lessors have to get more than one quote, etc, etc. But the easiest way is to create a management company in which each lessee is a shareholder (I say more about companies in the next chapter). The management company looks after the building and is run and funded by the lessees. They can then decide how and when they want the building maintained (subject to an overall obligation to the lessor to keep the building in good nick – after all, when it does revert he wants it to be still standing).

Commercial Leases

While we're on leases I just want to talk about commercial property. You and I understand and are familiar with residential property (houses and flats) because that's what we live in.

Commercial property is much more varied (shops, offices, restaurants, warehouses, factories, etc) but most commercial premises are leasehold. That's because businesses tend not to own the (freehold of the) buildings they occupy. Instead they rent them as tenants and the landlords tend to be big investment institutions such as pension funds and insurance companies for which commercial property is a major investment asset class. But for businesses, having their money tied up in property doesn't make much sense; far better to put that money to use in the business itself (by contrast the business of investment institutions is the owning, developing and letting out of property).

The business tenant will be concerned with **permitted use** (can I use these premises as a shop or restaurant?) while the landlord is principally concerned about whether the tenant might go bust (this is known as the strength of the **tenant's covenant** – you can see why now). So if a business is proposing to **assign** (sell or transfer) the lease to another business, the landlord may want the right to say no if the successor business is a weaker covenant.

This is why the assignment of a commercial lease will invariably be subject to the landlord's consent (the landlord will grant a **licence to assign**). But so the landlord can't hold an assignor to ransom, the lease usually says the landlord's consent is not to be **unreasonably withheld**. Property leases can be onerous things: if a business has taken out a 10-year lease it will be paying rent for the 10 years even if it moves out in the meantime, unless it can find a successor tenant to assign to. In fact there was a time when commercial leases had **upwards only** rent review clauses in them: every three years or so the landlord could revise the rent and put it up. Think about all of that the next time you go shopping.

Turnover Rents

You can see why commercial landlords like good business tenants and why they hate having premises empty. Empty premises (known as **voids**) are not producing income and are deteriorating.

In a shopping centre development, the big institutional landlord will try to attract an **anchor tenant** (a major name like a national supermarket or high street retailer) because then other smaller businesses will want to become tenants in the mall to benefit from the footfall (consumer traffic going past).

Equally the anchor tenant may only be prepared to pay a full rent if the mall is a success. So it may negotiate a **rent-free period** when the mall opens and may only be prepared to pay a **turnover rent** (a rent that reflects the amount of business it is getting).

At the end of the tenancy the business will have to make good any damage to the premises and reinstate them so they can be let by the landlord to the next business tenant. This is known as **dilapidations**: how much the landlord will charge the business by way of repairs to restore the premises once the tenancy ends and the business moves out.

This subject we're covering is known as landlord & tenant. The term **lease** and **tenancy** mean the same thing. But lease tends to apply to a long lease which can be bought and sold while a tenancy is a shorter period of occupation for which the tenant makes regular payments of rent.

Residential Tenancies

If the tenant pays rent every week he is said to have a weekly tenancy which he can give up (**surrender**) at a week's notice. Tenancies tend to be weekly, monthly or annual. The maintenance and insurance tend to be paid for by the landlord – the tenant doesn't feel he 'owns' the flat he's renting (which is why such tenancies often come furnished). Individuals and families on benefit will be housed by the local authority or housing associations (often set up as charities). Much of the law here is social housing law: disputes between tenants and local authorities over the state of premises and non-payment of rent; and additional **rights of occupation** (for instance, even when the tenancy has expired) so that a landlord can't just **evict** a tenant – these are called **statutory tenancies** because they are protected by Acts of Parliament (statutes).

Freehold

Why have I said so much about leases and flats and shops and tenancies, instead of starting with houses and freehold? Because we've now done the hard bit and the rest is easy. By contrast with landlord & tenant, freehold is straightforward. Disputes between freeholders tend to be over boundaries, trespass and nuisance.

So what I want to focus on in the rest of this chapter are two aspects of law affecting property that people live in: (1) land registration and (2) how houses are bought and sold (residential conveyancing).

Land Registration

It's generally held amongst lawyers who care about these things that the Law of Property Act 1925 is one of the most beautifully crafted pieces of parliamentary legislation ever (yes, 1925 yet again, the year of the trusts legislation from the last chapter: Sir Benjamin Cherry, a barrister, was the parliamentary draftsman behind all the 1925 legislation. His like will never be seen again).

The LPA25 (described by Megarry & Wade, the authoritative tome on land law, as 'without doubt the greatest single monument of legal wisdom, industry and ingenuity which the statute book can display') was designed to simplify title to land in order to make **land registration** possible. The Land Registration Act (also enacted in 1925; also the fruit of Cherry's labours) set out to simplify the way land is transferred.

Before the LRA25, title to land depended on the bundle of previous **conveyances** (a conveyance is a transfer of land), deeds, contracts and so on that the seller handed to you. As large estates fragmented and bits were sold off, these bits were subject to covenants and easements (an **easement** is a right of way over land, such as a footpath) in favour of the land retained. If settlements and trusts were also involved (remember the last chapter?) and there were leasehold interests (with which you're now familiar) too, you can see how it all began to become a mess. The only people who benefited were lawyers because buying and selling land was increasingly difficult and time-consuming so they charged more. Attempts to simplify all of this had been under discussion since the mid-nineteenth century. The only people against it were the lawyers.

So the LRA25 set up the Land Registry with the intention that in due course you could simply look at a central register to know everything important about a piece of land. Whatever was recorded at this registry would be definitive. To make this happen the LRA imposed a requirement of **first registration** which gradually extended to the whole country: so that whenever land in a given region was bought and sold after a particular date, the details had to be sent to the Land Registry for the land in question to be registered; after which it would be **registered land** and transferred (which replaced the term 'conveyed' for these purposes) using a simple piece of paper (a **transfer**) that referred to the details on the registry.

You can see that registered land has made the whole process of transferring property much, much easier and more certain. HIPs (Home Information Packs) were an extension of this idea, again to reduce the number of sales falling through. Instead they were abandoned soon after they were introduced because the housing market was depressed and they added to the cost of selling a home.

In the US they don't do any of this **investigation of title**. You see a house, you like it, you buy it, you move in. Simple. Over here you see a house, you get searches done, you come up to exchange of contracts, then you discover **defects in title** and you pull out. Or, worse still, the buyer from your buyer pulls out so leaving the chain high and dry. It causes delay and wasted expense. Chains of buyers and sellers collapse with each dependent on their buyer before they can themselves buy. No wonder in this country moving house is said to be as emotionally draining as divorce (and the cause of many).

(Incidentally this also gives rise to some other foolishness on the part of estate agents when they say enthusiastically: 'the property is sold with **vacant possession**'. What they mean is: 'the house is empty so there is no chain'. All properties are sold with vacant possession which means simply that on completion the buyer can move into an empty house. If a property doesn't have vacant possession it means there's a **sitting tenant** – a tenant who can't be evicted. You wouldn't want to buy that, would you?)

The way they do it in the US is that everyone has title insurance. If the title proves defective after you've moved in, an insurance company compensates you. It's rare. Since everyone is insured no one bothers to check title so the whole issue goes away.

Land registration has had a dramatic impact on property practice. In the old days, as I mentioned earlier, buying and selling a house was an expensive business: lawyers would charge a percentage of the **consideration** (that is, a fee that was a percentage of the price) – like estate agents. Nowadays it costs a few hundred pounds, not least because the government, in the interests of making house buying and selling quicker, easier and cheaper, opened up residential conveyancing to competition from **licensed conveyancers**. They may not know any or much other law but they certainly know enough land law to transfer title to a house (they do flats as well although flats can be more tricky for the reasons associated with leasehold mentioned earlier, and not least because every lease can be drafted differently; whereas freehold contracts and transfers are more standardised these days).

The impact on solicitors' firms over the last 20 years has been dramatic and has helped to change the face of legal practice. In the old days high street solicitors made a lot of money out of residential conveyancing and used it to offset (cross-subsidise) less profitable areas. They can't do that any more. As residential conveyancing has become easier so it has become much more of a process with 'legal factories' often attached to mortgage lenders springing up to do the legal work. A lot of this can be automated by computers generating standard letters and forms. Instead of solicitors, clerks can now do this work using computerised programs with dropdown menus and prompt questions. Some high street firms have gone out of business. Others, led by innovative, forward-thinking lawyers, have made fortunes by driving down costs, automating processes, charging less, competing on price and winning bulk business from mortgage lenders.

Land Law And Tort

In order for you to get a good, simple overview of law I am having to take some shortcuts and tell a few half-truths (but by the time you know what they are, this book will have served its purpose). So one thing I have tried to avoid is the way different branches of law overlap and interlink. I thought it would have freaked you earlier on. But now I think (given that you've got this far) that you're ready.

So although in this chapter we're dealing with land law, the other pillars of law can have an impact too. We've seen that already with equity (land held on trust). Now let's rewind a bit to tort (Chapter 2). The following are all types of tort that relate specifically to land (because land has been around forever, is valuable and, until we learn to fly or breathe underwater, is where we live).

Trespass to land conjures up pictures of people setting foot on others' land. But it's much wider than that. The merest physical contact is enough: my bike propped against your wall, my rubbish piled against your fence; both are trespass even though no damage is done (though what you might recover in court will be correspondingly small if you sue me). 'Land' includes the soil itself as well as anything under and above it, such as buildings and airspace – in fact anything needed for normal use and enjoyment of land. So, tunnelling under someone else's land is a trespass. Even swinging a crane *over* land can be: *Anchor Brewhouse v Berkley House* (1987).

Nuisance is about the unreasonable use of land that affects others' (usually neighbours') use of theirs. Originally, nuisance was a tort of strict liability – D was liable regardless of whether he was at fault (that is, regardless of whether he had done so deliberately, recklessly or without knowing at all). This is beginning to change so that nowadays D will only be liable if it was reasonably foreseeable that his unreasonable use of land would cause damage to the claimant's enjoyment of his or her own land.

Nuisance requires indirect interference (direct would be trespass) that causes damage and is unreasonable. It tends to be the result of a continuing state of affairs (a one-off incident is more likely to be trespass) and can range from damage caused by tree roots spreading into neighbouring property to flooding or even noise or smells.

Usually the damage is physical but it doesn't have to be: running a brothel in an otherwise respectable street was held to be nuisance in *Thompson-Schwab v Costaki* (1956) because of the emotional distress it caused. But disturbing a neighbour's pleasant view is not, because it's too ephemeral.

Whether the interference is unreasonable will depend on the location and how long it goes on for. In the case of *St Helens Smelting Co v Tipping* (1865) the court said that someone living in an industrial area could not complain about fumes from a copper works if they caused mere discomfort rather than actual damage to property (however, that was at the height of the Industrial Revolution). Just 14 years later, the court upheld a doctor's complaint against a confectionery maker who used industrial equipment in a street full of doctors' surgeries.

Neighbours' disputes over noise are frequent these days. Ironically, in *Christie v Davey* (1983) the person bringing the case (called the complainant) complained about the noise caused by his neighbour who was a music teacher and held musical parties. But the complainant was the one held by the court to be making the nuisance because he tried to disturb his neighbour's lessons and parties by making too much retaliatory noise himself.

Occupiers' Liability

Tortious liability can also be imposed by statute. One of the most interesting areas is what's called **occupiers' liability** (imposed by the Occupiers' Liability Act 1957 in relation to lawful visitors and by the Occupiers' Liability Act 1984 in relation to trespassers). Basically it says that landowners have to ensure their premises are safe for visitors. And that doesn't just mean lawful visitors (those invited on to the land, covered by OLA57). You have to look after unlawful visitors (trespassers) too (covered by OLA84).

It isn't enough just to put up a warning sign if that doesn't provide 'such care as in all the circumstances of the case is reasonable to see that the visitor will be reasonably safe in using the premises for the purposes for which he is invited or permitted to be there'. The duty is less onerous in the case of trespassers (the occupier has to be aware of the danger, the trespasser and the risk, for it to be reasonable to require the occupier to do anything). Cases range from children eating poisonous berries (occupier liable) to trespassing on railway lines (track owner not liable because it regularly repaired holes in fences through which kids tried to get in; but in another case a different railway company was liable because it was aware of a hole in a fence and kids' use of it, and did nothing about it). The Acts apply not just to land but to movable structures such as boats and planes.

There are some exceptions: for instance, in the case of persons 'exercising a calling' who implicitly are aware of risks inherent in what they do. So chimney sweeps dying from fumes from a boiler should have been aware of the dangers – *Roles v Nathan* (1963). However, the occupier is obliged to have checked out that the workmen are competent: in *Haseldine v Daw* (1941) an elevator engineer was killed in a lift. But there was no liability imposed on the building occupier since the engineer's employer was a competent firm. I imagine that this case was probably about whose insurer (the occupier's or the contractor's) should meet the claim from the dead man's estate. An awful lot of cases these days are really about which insurance company in the background should pick up the tab.

Rylands v Fletcher

There's one whole area of land-related tort that is simply (and bizarrely) named after the case that gave rise to it: *Rylands v Fletcher* (1868).

Whereas nuisance is about what you do *on* your land that affects others' enjoyment of theirs, **Rylands v Fletcher** is about what you allow to *escape from* your land that affects others. The case established that an occupier of land, who brings anything on to that land which is likely to cause damage if it escapes, is liable if that thing does escape and causes damage – regardless of whether the occupier was actually at fault or not (I suspect Frankenstein could have been sued for this, for allowing his creature to escape).

In *Rylands* itself D owned a mill and got a contractor to build a reservoir on his land to provide water for the mill. However, there were shafts on his land from an old coal mine that connected to the shafts of a neighbour's coal mine. The contractor could have blocked them up but didn't. Result: the reservoir flooded the neighbour's mine.

Now, the interesting thing – and compare this to *Donoghue v Stevenson* (the snail-in-the-bottle case) – is that the neighbour couldn't sue D for trespass (no direct damage) nor nuisance (it wasn't an ongoing situation); and the contractor had disappeared so wasn't around to be sued anyway. But the neighbour had obviously suffered damage because of what had happened. So the court ingeniously stepped in and established a new 'head of liability' as it's called. By the way, this is how law develops – which we'll come to in Chapter 10. Again, remember the year – 1868, when these sorts of industrial mishaps were increasingly likely.

So that's a ton of law relating to land that is actually tort. Now let's look at practice – at what real estate lawyers actually do.

Property-Related Areas Of Legal Practice

Residential conveyancing is the buying and selling of flats and houses.

Commercial property is about the development and management of buildings used in business, such as shops, shopping malls, warehouses and factories. It includes, at one end, site acquisition and, at the other, the letting of offices, warehouses and shops. Related areas of law include:

Planning (called 'zoning' in the US) which is about what you can build where. Local authorities grant **planning permission** and may require impact assessments on, for instance, local traffic. Often the developer may have to offer the local authority planning gain in return for planning permission, for instance a supermarket chain may have to provide affordable housing and local amenities like a swimming pool in return for permission to build an out-of-town megastore. Some major developments (such as airports) are subject to public inquiries that can go on for years and may in addition be subject to consent from central government. Planning lawyers are usually commercial property lawyers who decided to specialise further.

Construction (mentioned earlier) – building property developments.

Property finance – funding for property developments. The lending bank is called the **mortgagee**, not the mortgagor. The developer who's borrowing the money is the **mortgagor**. He's the one mortgaging the property as security for the promise to repay. The lender is the mortgagee, as the recipient of the promise to repay and the rights over the mortgaged property. The same applies in residential property: when you buy with a mortgage, you are the mortgagor because you mortgage the property to the lender, the mortgagee.

Landlord & tenant (L&T) is a big subset of property law since most commercial property is occupied by businesses as tenants. Since institutional investors often own hundreds and indeed thousands of properties, landlord & tenant at this level is often called property management. It is both non-contentious (drafting leases, licences to assign, notices, etc) and contentious (suing tenants, or being sued by landlords, for breach of covenant, service charge issues, dilapidations and forfeiture of leases). L&T is about acting for business tenants or their landlords. Individual (residential) tenants who get into disputes with their landlords tend to be poor so residential L&T is known as **housing** law which is part of **welfare** law.

Environment is closely related to planning and commercial property from which it first emerged as an area of law principally affecting land and the uses to which it is put. Originally, the first environmental lawyers tended to sit within planning and property departments of firms. That's now changed. Environmental law is a specialisation in its own right and the latest sub-specialisation is trading in carbon credits which is closely related to commodities. Environmental law is as likely to involve international carbon trading as it is industrial pollutants of rivers, for example. As global climate change leads to extreme weather and flooding so environmental law overlaps with regulatory law as well as litigation against builders, planning authorities, local and central government. Lawyers acting for related businesses (such as waste disposal and landfill) will often be lawyers specialising in commercial law.

Trespass, nuisance and occupiers' liability are property-related torts mentioned above. Neighbour disputes over boundaries can also give rise to litigation.

Equity (trusts law) is highly relevant to property law. We saw that when two or more people own property they hold that property on what is called a trust for sale. They are empowered to sell the property and to hold it as trustees in the meantime with themselves as the beneficiaries. They can hold as joint tenants (so each is entitled to the whole property) or they can sever (split) that joint tenancy and become tenants in common instead (so each is entitled to one half of the property).

Trusts law is also relevant to commercial property and, in particular, investment in commercial property. I mentioned earlier that big financial institutions such as pension funds and insurance companies are major investors in commercial property. But, like all property, commercial property can be difficult to sell and these institutional investors are used to being able to trade in and out of assets such as shares and bonds. However, if a building is owned by a **REIT** (**real estate investment trust**) then investors can buy (and sell) units in the holding trust rather than having to buy and sell the underlying building itself. This makes commercial property a more liquid investment (one that is easier to move in and out of) which in turn makes it more attractive.

And Finally...

Rights Above And Below The Ground

In this chapter I've ignored rights above and below the land itself. Above the land there are rights to light (so neighbours can't block out your light by building a skyscraper right up against your wall). Rights attached to river banks (such as fishing) are riparian rights. Rights below the surface include mineral rights and rights of extraction – hugely valuable to water, oil and mining companies.

Two Terms Of Art In Property Law

Caveat emptor (mentioned earlier) means 'buyer beware' and is the general principle that in property law the buyer has to satisfy him- or herself that the seller has title. It used to be absolute but now when you sell a flat or house you have to make certain disclosures to the buyer that if you fail to can be actionable.

Adverse possession is a way of establishing legal title to land just by dint of occupying it. You have to do so for a long time (a decade at least) and in such a way that people know that you are. If after all that time no one objects you can swear an **affidavit** (or 'happydavid' as I've also heard it called) which is a sworn statement confirming the period of your occupation of the identified piece of land without interference from anyone else. This will confer legal title on you. It is pretty rare but ensures that strips of land don't fall off the radar and then block redevelopment because no one knows who owns them.

So far I've mentioned businesses on and off. Businesses are mainly (but not always) companies. Which is what we're going to look at next. However, we've now covered what I believe to be the fundamentals, the pillars, of law: crime, tort, contract, property and trusts (equity).

CHAPTER 7

COMPANY LAW

Sole trader – partnership – company – limited liability – insolvent –
bankrupt – joint and several liability – limited liability partnerships (LLPs) –
corporate veil – private clients – equity finance – mergers & acquisitions
(M&A) – listing – private equity – financial services – investment funds –
debt finance – loans – bonds – capital markets – security – banking –
syndicated lending – asset finance – project finance – construction –
insolvency – company law – City law firms – in-house lawyers

Company law is the backbone of business. If you want to set up in business, there are various ways you can do it. You can be a **sole trader** working on your own in your own name. You can be in **partnership** with others. Or you can form a **company**. Forming a company costs as little as £20. You can tell when a business is a company because it has the word 'Limited' or 'Ltd' after its name (or even PLC for 'Public Limited Company' if it is a larger company with, or aiming to have, more than 50 shareholders).

Limited Liability

The one advantage that a company has over a sole trader or a partnership is **limited liability**. This means that if a company goes bust (becomes **insolvent** and ceases to trade) the directors running the company won't be liable for its debts; and the shareholders won't have to put in any more money if they've already paid for their shares (of course they won't get their money back either). Limited liability is hugely important for business. It encourages people to be entrepreneurial: to back new inventions or innovations without worrying whether they are risking all they own.

By contrast, a sole trader or the partners in a partnership will be liable for their business debts until those have been paid off unless they go **bankrupt** in the meantime (note on legal language: companies become insolvent; individuals become bankrupt). In a partnership the partners have **joint and several liability** for the business debts. Joint means that they are all equally liable. Several means each is liable for the entire debt. This means that if, say, one partner makes a mistake and is sued for negligence, everyone shares in the liability (joint) and any one of them can be required to meet the full amount of it (several). This means that partners could lose all they own if a partnership goes bust.

Because of this, **limited liability partnerships** (**LLPs**) were introduced to allow big firms of lawyers, accountants and other professionals, who have traditionally traded as partnerships but are now international businesses, to get the benefit of limited liability. An LLP is a cross between a partnership and a company. (As mentioned previously, partnerships also take out professional indemnity insurance to protect against liability for negligence.)

Limited liability was introduced by the Joint Stock Companies Act 1844 at the height of the Industrial Revolution. There had been companies before – such as the East India Company and the company behind the South Sea Bubble – but these tended to be one-offs, each created by a specific Act of Parliament for a particular purpose with its own charter. In other words, they were still pretty unusual. Nowadays anyone can form a company and do almost anything or nothing with it.

What's so special about a company? The House of Lords in 1897 heard a case called *Salomon v Salomon*, described by Harry Street in his famous book *Freedom, The Individual And The Law* as 'the sheet-anchor of the modern law of incorporated companies' which means it's a biggy.

Mr Salomon had a company called Salomon Limited in which he owned virtually all of the issued shares. He lent the company money and took out security for the loan in the form of a debenture (like a property mortgage, but over the company's assets). This meant that he had priority over other creditors. He could get his money back first. The company became insolvent (went bust) and he insisted that the debenture meant he should be repaid in full before anyone else.

You can see what happened. All the other creditors cried foul and said that he and his company were effectively the same thing so his claim should be ignored.

But the House of Lords disagreed and said: no, his company is a separate arm's length entity so his claim stands.

This was hugely important because it meant individuals could be separated from their businesses if they conducted the latter through companies. The law treats a company as an entity that is separate from its owners and directors. This separation of a company from its directors and shareholders is called the **corporate veil**. Just occasionally the courts will coyly 'lift the corporate veil' and hold the directors personally liable for the company's debts but that's quite unusual and tends to be for things like fraud or continuing to trade when you know the company is insolvent.

You can begin to see now the big step forward that business took when the Joint Stock Companies Act was introduced. Sign a bit of paper, as Mr Salomon did, pay a start-up fee and an annual fee, file records regularly with Companies House, and you are shielded from liability. Sounds simple, doesn't it? Well, the latest incarnation of the Companies Act dates from 2006 and runs to almost 700 pages.

At its heart, corporate law establishes two things. First, shareholders aren't liable for the debts of the companies they invest in, over and above their equity investment. This is important because they wouldn't invest if they could lose more than they put in. This means they don't have to be so concerned about the running of the business which is why, second, companies are run by directors who don't have to be shareholders. Directors themselves are only liable if they do something really stupid or fraudulent (gross misfeasance).

Limited liability is key to encouraging entrepreneurs. The equity funding provided to start-ups is called 'venture capital' because it is risk capital. Without entrepreneurs there is no innovation and no pipeline of new businesses to replace those that are taken over or wither and die from being outmoded. This is why the courts are highly reluctant to go behind the screen of limited liability (by lifting the corporate veil) and hesitate to impose liability for a company's debts on its directors and, even less so, its shareholders.

That's not to say that relations between shareholders and directors are always cordial: one reason for a lot of the stuff in the Companies Act is to regulate relations between them.

Corporate Lawyers v Private Client Lawyers

This development of company law was also significant for the development of law and lawyers.

Till 1844, all clients were individuals (what lawyers now call **private clients**). They were individual people and families. But as the use of companies became widespread, companies became a new type of client in their own right. This didn't happen overnight because the first companies were set up and run by the individuals who owned them, so the individual and the company were pretty much the same (hence a case like *Salomon*).

But as companies grew they started to go public (that is, to list on the London Stock Exchange) and to attract a wider group of shareholders who looked to the board of directors (whom they appointed) to run the company in their (the shareholders') best interests. So, over time, companies developed as entities separate from their owners. This is why law firms in the City of London (where the Stock Exchange is) started to specialise in acting for companies and over time became too expensive to act for individuals.

Nowadays companies listed on the London Stock Exchange are owned in the main by institutional shareholders such as pension funds, insurance companies and investment funds – the very institutions that own all that commercial property in the last chapter. And company law (as you saw from the size of the most recent legislation) is a legal specialisation in its own right.

Equity v Debt

Nowadays the engine room of a major City law firm comprises equity and debt finance.

Equity finance is about companies (1) listing their shares on the London Stock Exchange and (2) taking each other over (the collective name for takeovers is **mergers & acquisitions** or **M&A**).

Listing is also known as 'going public' or doing an 'IPO' (which stands for 'initial public offering') or 'floating' or doing a 'flotation'. It means that a company's shares are now available widely and can be bought and sold on the Stock Exchange.

Equity finance also covers M&A because it's easier to take over another company once you have gone public yourself because you can use your shares to pay for the acquisition (the shareholders in the target company you are taking over give you their shares in the target in return for shares in you) so shares are often at the heart of M&A deals.

Another part of equity finance is **private equity**, which is about raising money from big investment institutions to take over public companies, break them up, sell off bits and refloat the rest.

In terms of the impact on City law firms, M&As led the way. The first UK takeover took place in the late 1950s and it marked the start of the switch by law firms from acting for individuals to acting for companies – helped by the lifting of the 20-partner ceiling in 1967 which meant that firms could grow in order to provide teams of lawyers providing highly complex advice in big transactions. This meant that by the 1980s most large City law firms had exited from private client work altogether. However, there are still mid-sized firms in central London doing private client work successfully, but they also tend to do corporate work too.

The actual law involved is a combination of company law (under the Companies Acts), financial services law, Stock Exchange regulations and Takeover Panel rules (the Takeover Panel is the body that polices M&As) as set out in the Takeover Code. **Financial services** includes **investment funds**, that is, the creation of investment funds such as unit trusts, their regulation and the marketing of them to the public. Any attempt to raise money by way of public issues (such as promoting shares to the public for them to buy) is heavily regulated to avoid fraud. Much of it concerns the detail of what an investment manager or promoter of a fund or issue can and can't say when marketing that issue.

Debt finance is about (1) **loans** (banks lending to corporate borrowers) and (2) **bonds**. Bonds are IOUs issued by companies and governments for big amounts – sometimes more than a billion dollars at a time. They too are bought by institutional investors.

Bank lending is done by commercial banks. Bond issuance is assisted by investment banks. It's these investment banks that also help companies float which is why the two activities of issuing shares (equity) and bonds (debt) are often grouped together under the heading of **capital markets.**

Debt finance is a huge area of law (especially internationally where English and New York law are the dominant systems) and forms the core practice of many of the world's largest law firms. Again it is based on contract but much specialist law has developed around the taking of **security** (the lender taking a charge over the borrower's assets in order to be able to sell them to recover the debt if the borrower fails to repay it, a bit like property mortgages in the last chapter). This includes the law around guarantees and sureties. This is where **banking** law shades into insolvency (see below).

Some areas related to debt finance include: **syndicated lending** (where more than one bank lends to a single borrower, using one loan agreement); **asset finance** (aka finance leasing or equipment leasing) which is a way of financing big things like planes and ships where the bank owns the asset and rents it to the business that wants to use it; and **project finance**, which is about funding infrastructure developments, from power stations, dams, roads, harbours and airports to train stations, hospitals and schools. It allows for the fact that these projects can take years to complete before there is any payback. It overlaps with **construction** and engineering.

Big City law firms do both equity finance and debt finance work. Perhaps the defining moment for City practice was the merger in 1989 between two large firms, one noted for its corporate (equity) work, the other for its banking (debt) work, to create Clifford Chance, one of the largest law firms in the world.

Other Related Areas

Insolvency is the law that applies when a business goes bust. Law firms that do banking often also do insolvency, advising their banking clients on how to recover loans made to companies that subsequently become insolvent (which is why the companies can't repay them). It's a technically demanding area of law that lays down who gets what, in which order, when a business ceases. The challenge is that there are usually fewer assets than there are claims, and lenders tend to have competing interests.

Company law is, as mentioned above, the law relating to the establishment and running of companies including the rights of shareholders and the duties of directors. Every so often the government revises company law. Recent revisions have included the Companies Acts of 1948, 1967, 1985 and, most recently, 2006.

Of course these aren't the only things these big City firms do but company law, equity and debt finance are core. **City law firms** do a load of other things too. Many of these flow from M&A work, such as competition law (relevant when companies risk becoming market dominant through takeovers), employment and pensions (when you're acquiring another workforce), tax (to structure the deal efficiently), intellectual property (if the target company has valuable brands and trademarks), commercial (checking out its contracts), property (ditto its premises) and so on. All of these are relevant to something called 'due diligence' which is checking whether a company that is going public or being taken over is all it appears to be.

All of these specialisations are relevant to takeovers but corporate clients will also seek this specialist advice in connection with their day-to-day business.

While we're on the subject of companies, there are lawyers, called **in-house lawyers**, who work in legal departments within companies (and banks). They may have trained as solicitors or barristers but decided to go in-house in order to be closer to the commercial world. The big companies and banks they work for come from, and do business, all over the world. The City of London is itself a top international financial centre. So although we've been looking at our own (English common) law, it's now time to look further afield.

CHAPTER 8

COMPARATIVE LAW

International – jurisdictions – comparative law – Roman law – civil law – common law – Anglo-Saxon – codified – adversarial – inquisitorial – persuasive – conflicts of laws – choice of law – choice of forum – boilerplate – private international law – nexus – lex fori – lex loci actus – lex situs – public international law – European law – shipping – commodities – energy, oil and gas – upstream – downstream – insurance and reinsurance – international trade – ab initio – carpe diem – caveat emptor – contra proferentem – habeas corpus – ignorantia non excusat lex – novus actus interveniens – obiter dictum – quis custodiet ipsos custodes – res ipsa loquitur – scintilla temporis – uberrimei fidei – volenti non fit injuria – void – voidable

We saw in the last chapter what City law firms do – corporate and finance work – but the largest law firms don't just practise English law. They have offices all over the world and are very much **international** law firms. So it's time to look beyond our national horizons at the laws of other countries (**jurisdictions** as they are called). The study of the laws of more than one jurisdiction is called **comparative law**.

Civil Law (Roman Law)

The story starts (as do so many things) with the Romans. The Roman emperor Justinian must have been very boring or very enlightened or maybe he just had a lot of time on his hands because one of the biggest acts of his reign was to have all of **Roman law** written down (codified) in books called collectively the Justinian Code. A millennium or so later, another emperor (Napoleon) followed his example and did the same to French law, creating the Code Napoléon which is based on the Justinian Code.

France isn't the only country to have done this. Most western European countries are also **civil law** countries, that is, their law is based on the Roman civil code (here 'civil' comes from the Roman for 'citizen' and in this context means roughly 'civic'). They include Spain, Germany, the Netherlands and Belgium as well as France – and from there it has spread to former colonies and dominions throughout Africa, Asia and Latin America. In Germany, Roman law itself was actually in force until the introduction of the German civil code in 1900. A branch now known as Roman-Dutch law is the basis of South African law.

Civil Law v Common Law

By contrast, English law is **common law**. English law developed as the body of law applied in court in cases in which the king didn't have a direct interest (hence 'common'). It is also known as **Anglo-Saxon** law because its principles were exported via the British Empire to Hong Kong, Australia, New Zealand, Canada and the US. Within the context of common law the term 'civil law' is used to mean the law between citizens (such as contract, tort and so on) as opposed to criminal law which is imposed on the citizen by the state.

So civil law has two meanings: in English law, civil as opposed to criminal; and internationally, civil law as opposed to common law.

Adversarial v Inquisitorial

The basic difference is that common law develops piecemeal through cases and legislation. By contrast civil law is based on a set of laws which are **codified** (set out in a single code). It feeds through into the underlying legal culture. Under common law you can do something unless the law says otherwise. Under civil law you can't unless the code allows it.

It's also fundamental to the role of courts and judges. In common law courts the two parties argue between them and the judge decides on the basis of those arguments (this is known as the **adversarial** system). The idea is that justice is forged out of the collision of opposing arguments. By contrast in civil courts the judge has an **inquisitorial** role. He establishes the facts by questioning the parties and so arrives at the truth.

However, these differences can be exaggerated. Large parts of common law are in effect codified by successive statutes. The civil code for its part isn't comprehensive. Cases that are meant simply to interpret it end up having precedential value and adding to it. But there can be differences. For instance, under English law you cannot have an agreement to agree (that is, a binding agreement to enter into an agreement): you've either entered into one or you haven't. Not so in civil law jurisdictions where an agreement to enter into an agreement is itself binding. Equally, in civil law there is a duty to negotiate in good faith which, if breached, enables the wronged party to set the agreement aside. Not so in common law where anything goes (unless it's an actual misrepresentation which is itself actionable).

The point is that every country has its own legal system. So, for example, cases in common law jurisdictions don't have precedential value in other common law countries because technically each of these countries has its own system of laws and is a separate jurisdiction. But because their laws all have a common ancestry, such cases are said to have **persuasive** value – courts may look at them and choose to be influenced by them if they want.

New York Law And English Law

International legal practice is actually dominated by the laws of England and New York and this is why the biggest law firms in the world are UK and US law firms with offices throughout the globe. I mentioned in the last chapter that the principal areas of practice for the biggest law firms are corporate and finance. The biggest deals in these fields tend to be done under New York or English law. I say 'New York' because there is no actual 'American law': there is state law and then federal law but no single national set of laws. And I say 'English': there's no such thing as 'UK law' either. Strictly speaking it's the laws of England and Wales. Scotland and Northern Ireland have their own systems, although they are similar and nowadays lawyers as a shorthand will refer to 'UK law' meaning the law of England and Wales.

There are two reasons for this dominance. In the case of English law, it's historic: English law followed the spread of Britain's trading empire; English courts were regarded as impartial; and English became the international business language. So English law became a popular choice amongst international traders. In the case of New York it's current: that's where the money and the biggest banks are; when they do deals they do them under New York law.

Choice Of Law

But as things become more global and people and businesses cross borders, so the potential for systems of law to rub up against each other increases. This is called **conflicts of laws**.

One way of avoiding such conflicts, at least in contract, is to make sure that in the agreement the parties choose which system of laws they want to govern the contract (**choice of law**) and which country's courts should adjudicate any dispute (**choice of forum**). It's perfectly possible for, say, Swiss courts to hear a case involving the application of English law. The Swiss court will probably want to hear expert evidence to establish what precisely the relevant English law in the particular case is. Clauses in contracts dealing with these sorts of issues are called **boilerplate**: they're standard, they have nothing to do with the substance of the agreement, but you need them in there.

Comparative Law

As you can imagine, the law governing conflicts of laws is complex. You may be surprised that there is no such thing as international law as such (one set of rules that applies all over the world) although there are some international conventions which establish rules that parties can decide to apply to their transaction.

This is especially so in international trade and shipping where UNCITRAL (the United Nations Commission on International Trade Law) is a popular choice, just as in the US there is the US Uniform Commercial Code. These are sets of laws that parties can choose to have apply to their contract. Why would they do so? Ease and certainty: much better for both parties to choose a tried-and-tested set of rules to govern their commercial relationship rather than leave it up in the air.

Private International Law

If it is left up in the air, the parties have to resort to something called **private international law** (another term for conflicts of laws) which is the set of rules that determines which of two competing jurisdictions (systems of law) applies. It's what that Swiss court would try to do if the contract didn't mention English law or any governing law at all.

Different jurisdictions have different rules for resolving this but in general they look for **nexus** (connection) or contiguity – what touch-points does an agreement or the parties to it have to a particular jurisdiction. The relevant factors include: where it was concluded; where it is to be performed; where the parties are located, etc, etc.

If there is doubt about the applicable law (for instance there isn't a choice of law clause in the agreement or the dispute involves a tort rather than a contract) a court will apply **lex fori** (that is, the law of the forum, meaning the law of the court before which the case is heard) to all procedural issues (including the choice of law rules). If it's a tort then the choice of law will be heavily influenced by where the tort took place (**lex loci actus** – 'locus' is Latin for 'place' hence the words 'local' and 'location') and that country's laws are most likely to apply. If, for example, it's a dispute involving land, then the **lex situs** (where the land is 'sited' – situated) is most likely to apply. And so on.

Public International Law

By contrast, **public international law** is the law that applies between countries to resolve disputes between them. It covers things like countries' borders with each other, the law of the seabed as well as vexed questions such as when is war legal.

The first is called private because it affects the rights of individual citizens. The second is public because it affects relations between states.

One of the sources of public international law is treaties. Organisations created by inter-state treaty include the United Nations (formed out of the ashes of the 1939-45 war) and the International Court of Justice in The Hague to which states can submit disputes by mutual consent. Other significant treaties include the European Convention on Human Rights 1950 (that's not its full title but is the one by which it is best known) which established the European Court of Human Rights.

European Law

Talk of Europe brings us to **European law** to which the UK has been subject since 1973 when it joined the European Economic Community, now subsumed within the European Union (EU). There are different strands of EU law – treaties, directives, regulations, declarations and conventions to name just a few – and they take effect in different ways, either directly without anything further or indirectly by an enabling Act of Parliament.

How and to what extent EU law takes effect in the UK has provoked many cases and much discussion amongst lawyers, as has the fact that UK courts have the power to refer questions on EU law to the European Court of Justice. EU law overrides UK law where the two are inconsistent and the UK is under a duty not to enact legislation at odds with EU law. This has the knock-on effect that, if in doubt, the courts will interpret Acts of Parliament to comply with EU law. However, the UK courts are not required to distort UK law to enforce against an individual an EU directive that has no direct effect between individuals, and so on, and so on.

Even Denning got in on the act, stating in *H P Bulmer v J Bollinger* (1974) that an English judge has complete discretion to refer to the European Court of Justice a question on the interpretation of (what is now called) EU law and drawing a clear distinction between interpreting the law and applying it. The European Court of Justice can do the former but not the latter so it can't declare national law invalid or reverse the judgments of national courts (while nevertheless trying to impose consistency in the application of EU law across member states). For me, what's interesting about that case is why a cider maker and a champagne producer were in court at all (it was over use of the term 'champagne' in a Babycham advert).

In the main, although EU law has had increasing impact in member states it's really about creating a level playing field (hence 'common market') for goods and services so they can be sold without modification across member states and labour can move freely. It's also about preventing cartels and monopolies which would work against a level playing field – which is why for UK lawyers a lot of EU law is really competition law which affects companies taking each other over (M&A – see previous chapter).

But it also affects things like: customs duties; agriculture; free movement of services and capital; restrictive trade practices; and the regulation of particular industries such as the coal, steel and nuclear industries.

Most domestic law has remained unaffected such as criminal, contract, tort, real estate and so on. But that may change following the European Commission's interest in establishing uniform cross-border laws in the consumer and insurance sectors.

International Legal Practice

Although all transactions (contracts) and disputes (cases) are jurisdiction-specific (ultimately governed by the laws of one country) there are some areas of practice that are necessarily international because they involve parties from different countries. Here are some examples:

Shipping traditionally involves 'wet admiralty' (the law about collisions between ships) and 'dry admiralty' (the law surrounding the transport of cargo). Both have their own terminology. 'Salvage' concerns the rights of those who rescue cargo (and the wreck itself) when a ship sinks. 'Freight' is the charge for carrying goods. Some shipping contracts are 'cif' (carriage, insurance and freight included) and some are 'fob' (free on board) – the differences concern who pays for what. A 'bill of lading' is a crucial document: it is evidence of the contract of carriage, is receipt for the goods and evidence of title to the goods – this last means the goods can be sold on while still at sea.

Since shipping is almost by definition international, it is also necessarily about international trade which is why it also overlaps with commodities law and international trade law (UNCITRAL – see above). Shipping is also related to insurance and reinsurance.

Commodities are goods that are transported round the world, ranging from hard commodities like steel to soft commodities – foodstuffs like sugar, coffee, tea and cocoa. Most commodities are traded on commodity exchanges or simply between parties in what is called the spot market. Commodities law applies to such transactions but extends to the transport and insurance of commodities (see shipping and international trade). Such deals are often financed through trade finance which is an aspect of banking law.

A small number of substantial London law firms specialise almost exclusively in shipping, international trade and commodities law.

Energy, oil and gas law is typical of sector-specific areas of law that have developed over the past few decades (shipping and banking being amongst the earliest). This area of law divides into two: upstream and downstream activities. **Upstream** is about getting the oil and gas out of the ground or, in the case of electricity, generating it. It can cross over with project finance and includes mining rights and other contractual relations between governments, landowners and businesses involved in extracting, generating and transport. Oil pipelines that run for hundreds of miles across inhospitable territory require construction agreements, licences and distribution agreements. **Downstream** activity is about marketing, selling, distributing and transporting energy, as well as health & safety and other regulatory aspects. This sort of work tends to be the preserve of the larger law firms because it draws upon so many specialisations.

Insurance and reinsurance is closely linked to shipping. It isn't so much about the primary insurance market (where individuals and businesses take out insurance cover) but about the contracts that insurers take out with reinsurers to offload some of the risk they have underwritten. Reinsurance is an international business, much of it carried on in London (Lloyd's of London is the world's biggest reinsurance market) so contracts and claims tend to be international. Much of the work is litigious (that is, about taking cases to court) because large claims are almost always resisted. It's an area of law that has its own language ('cedants', 'retrocessionaires', 'treaties', 'facultative') and is closely linked to shipping because the maritime world is one of the biggest users of insurance (for ships and cargoes).

International trade overlaps with shipping since it involves contracts for the cross-border supply of goods and commodities, usually involving transport and insurance considerations.

Coda

Just to finish off and since we've covered Roman law in this chapter, here are a few Latin legalisms ('coda' is itself from the Latin word 'cauda' meaning 'tail'):

Ab initio From the start (so 'void ab initio' means that something isn't legally binding at all)

Carpe diem 'Seize the day' but famous amongst lawyers as the name of the dominant time recording app

Caveat emptor Buyer beware (it's up to the buyer to make checks)

Contra proferentem Against the proposer: this means, for example, that an exclusion clause in a contract will be interpreted 'against' the person seeking to rely on it, in other words, narrowly

Habeas corpus You have the body (that is, the person should be released)

Ignorantia non excusat lex The law doesn't excuse ignorance, that is, ignorance of the law is no defence

Novus actus interveniens New act intervening (meaning that the chain of causation is broken)

Obiter dictum (also just 'obiter') Statement by a judge that isn't binding because not strictly on the point in dispute

Quis custodiet ipsos custodes Who judges the judges (literally: who acts as custodian of the custodians) meaning: what checks are there on those in power?

Res ipsa loquitur The thing speaks for itself (used where no further evidence is required other than the fact of the incident itself)

Scintilla temporis A brief moment in time

Uberrimei fidei Utmost good faith (an important concept in insurance law where failure to make complete disclosure of all pertinent facts can invalidate the policy)

Volenti non fit injuria Willingness to accept the risk removes liability (injury)

English law has its own phrases, such as: 'reasonable man' (an objective test of what rational, ethical ordinary people might think or do in similar circumstances), 'the man on the Clapham omnibus' (old-fashioned version of the same), 'with clean hands' (as you know, an expression from equity meaning that you can't invoke equity as a principle of fairness if you have acted unfairly yourself), 'not to be unreasonably withheld' (this applies to consents – for example, the landlord's consent to the transfer of a lease) and, a personal favourite this, 'bona fide third-party purchaser for value without notice' – a buyer who gets good title from a seller even though the seller wasn't entitled to sell. The terms 'void' and 'voidable' cause confusion. **Void** means that something (usually a contract) is a nullity from the start ('void ab initio' – meaning void from initiation, as above – is the full term).

Voidable means that it can be treated as being of no effect by one of the parties if they wish.

The reason for this emphasis on words is that lawyers, as we've seen, are good with language. They have to be. They draw up agreements. In litigation they pore over the other side's claim, picking holes in its arguments. Now we're going to see what else they need to be good at. We're going to look at the business of law.

CHAPTER 9

LAW IN PRACTICE: LAWYERS

Agreements – contentious – litigators – litigation – non-contentious – knowledge management – value add – associates – partners – Solicitors Regulation Authority (SRA) – business development (BD) – client relationship management (CRM) – pitch for business – invitation to tender (ITT) – request for particulars (RFP) – panel of law firms – time spent – fixed fees – pricing – six pillars of pricing – value for money (VFM) – Stephen Mayson – RULES of profitability – headline rate – discount – volume discount – moral editing – write down – written off – realised rate – utilisation – chargeable time – leverage – gearing – expenses – variable costs – speed – cash flow – working capital – paid on account – interim billing – work-in-progress (WIP) – debtors – David Maister – 3Es – expertise – experience – efficiency – extinction – partnership retreat – offsite – mentor – solicitor – barrister – legal executive – paralegals – licensed conveyancers – patent attorneys – trademark agents – notaries – scriveners – in-house lawyers – general counsel – business services – support staff – sole practitioners – sole principals – legal aid firms – high street firms – medium sized firms – regional firms – national firms – City law firms – international law firms – magic circle

If you walk around a firm of solicitors you'll see any or all of the following: lawyers behind desks, poring over documents; lawyers on the phone; lawyers sitting in front of their monitors typing or answering emails; lawyers in meetings; and lawyers in each other's offices discussing points of law. So what do lawyers do all day? Basically, I think they do ten things.

1. Researching The Law

You will have seen (I hope) that it's often not easy to say what the law actually is (large parts of it are in a bit of a muddle) or to apply it to the client's particular facts or circumstances. Even if it is, you need to make sure you're up-to-date and aware of the latest cases and statutes in an area. So research (looking up the law online or in a law firm library) is an important part of a lawyer's working life and the more junior you are the more research you tend to do, at the request of the more senior lawyers in a firm. I won't say any more about research: the bulk of this book so far has been about the law and it's barely scratched the surface.

2. Drafting Legal Documents

Legal documents fall into two broad categories, those relating to disputes and those relating to agreements. Work relating to disputes is called **contentious** work. It's about preparing cases to be heard in court and the lawyers – barristers and solicitors – who do this tend to be known as **litigators** since contentious work is also called **litigation** or dispute resolution. Work that isn't about disputes is called **non-contentious**. It's generally about putting together agreements.

The drafting of agreements and of papers for court (claims, defences, witness statements and so on) is a key skill. It requires the use of English but not of the sort you and I use to talk. It has to be clear, comprehensive, often exhaustive and usually technical. As one lawyer once told me: 'In an agreement you are legislating for the future, covering every possible eventuality so that everyone involved knows where they stand.' That's why agreements can be very long and extremely turgid to read. You don't read a contract the way you read John Grisham (himself a former lawyer).

In most large law firms there are banks of precedents and templates to help lawyers draft agreements (it's the bit of a large law firm called **knowledge management**). The skill then lies in what is called free-hand drafting. Suppose the parties to a transaction come up with a novel pricing mechanism at two in the morning and turn to you as the lawyer in the room to reduce what they have devised to paper. Could you do that in a way that stands up to scrutiny, that will be the blueprint for them to follow in everyday business, that if necessary will be upheld by a court if they ever fall out over it in years to come? You can begin to see why lawyers need to be able to cope with pressure.

3. Advising Clients

This is about helping the client deal with whatever issue they face. It means knowing the law but, as importantly, knowing what to do with and about it to help your client. Clients don't pay lawyers a lot of money just to be told: 'This is what the law is and, no, sorry, you can't do what you were proposing to.' These days clients want (to use that awful cliché) solutions. They also don't have much time for lawyers who say: 'Well, on the one hand you could do this and on the other you could do that.' They want the lawyer to use his or her experience of other similar situations to know what the client should do here. Clients value this ability more than they value legal expertise (most clients can't tell whether a lawyer is good or not at law; but they can certainly tell whether a lawyer is valuable to them in terms of analysing the issues and weighing up different possible outcomes). This is a lawyer or law firm's **value add** (another BD cliché).

4. Negotiating With The Other Side

You can probably see that negotiation is key to resolving disputes which would otherwise end up in court (litigation or contentious practice). But it's equally important in non-contentious work (concluding agreements). Whether a lawyer is helping a client buy a house or negotiating a multi-billion pound corporate M&A deal, he or she will spend a lot of time negotiating terms with the lawyer 'on the other side'. Of course, the popular view of negotiating is that it's all about driving a hard bargain, being tough, slamming your fist down on the table and being prepared to walk out. It's none of that. It's actually about exploring what each side wants and seeing how it can be accommodated. You'd be surprised how often what each side wants is perfectly acceptable to the other provided their issues and concerns are accommodated in turn. Even price becomes a mechanism for regulating these wider aspects. Lawyers will tell you that negotiation is about allocating risk: where should a risk fall if it occurs? Of course, a dispute, whether or not it gets to court, is all about negotiation and if it gets to court that's usually indicative of the failure of the negotiation process. Individuals may want their day in court but businesses generally just want money.

5. Communicating With Clients And The Other Side

This is about being good with language. Lawyers tend to be good with words and good at grammar. This is the language used to draft documents. It's legal, technical English. But lawyers also need to be good at English as it is usually written and spoken. The problem is that many lawyers forget to switch from one to the other which is why they often come across as stilted, pompous and boring. The best letter I've ever seen written by a lawyer to his client was one line long: 'You were right and I was wrong.' The worst was a 10-page letter which ended with the statement: 'So that's the answer but I'm still not sure why you asked me this particular question.'

All of the above elements probably seem pretty obvious. They tend to be done by **associates** – qualified solicitors who aren't (yet) partners. But as they become **partners** (who are the owners of the firms they work in) they will spend an increasing amount of their time on the following activities.

6.   Structuring And Strategising

For big companies and banks, doing deals and dealing with disputes is endemic to business. So they want lawyers who will devise transaction structures to minimise commercial risk and mitigate regulatory issues or (in litigation) plot a strategy that will bring a dispute to a satisfactory conclusion. Big corporate transactions (such as takeovers) and financial transactions (such as project financings) generate scores of agreements, some running to several hundred pages. Equally, court cases can generate van-loads of documents. None of this is any good unless there is an underlying structure, plan or strategy that the lawyer is on top of.

7.   Managing Matters

It follows from the previous item that lawyers leading big transactions and disputes have to project manage those matters to a successful conclusion: they have to drive them forward, often to tight and demanding deadlines set by clients for tax and accounting purposes. In the largest firms it is not uncommon to have 50-100 lawyers working on different aspects of the same deal, each team applying a different legal specialisation often in different offices applying the law of the local jurisdiction. Bringing these people together, coordinating their work and output and keeping in daily contact with the client is a full-time job in its own right. Senior lawyers acting in big deals or disputes don't do much straightforward legal work as such. Instead, they are project managing, often across teams and offices.

8.   Managing Others

What makes any business or profession both interesting and demanding is the fact that you are dealing with people in all their myriad varieties and challenges. Lawyers rarely work on their own these days. Even in a small firm a partner will be managing a secretary or PA and a junior lawyer. As a lawyer you have to learn to delegate to, and manage, others in order to get them to do what you need done. If you thought law was about sitting in an ivory tower all day researching complex legal issues, well, it is occasionally like that. But it's no refuge for those who don't want to deal with people.

9. Making A Profit

Nor is law a refuge for those who don't like business. As a lawyer you are in business, even if the clients you serve are individuals for whom you are conveying houses or drawing up wills or negotiating divorces. Whatever you are doing you need to do at a profit, otherwise you will go out of business. Besides, business clients expect their lawyers to understand the rudiments of accounts and to talk to them about how much the legal advice will cost. So lawyers need to be able to run matters to a profit and to make sure the firm itself is properly managed. Without cash flow, a law firm will go bust; without profit it won't prosper.

10. Developing The Business

Partners get involved in managing and developing their firm. This includes areas such as the recruitment and training of young lawyers, developing a firm's legal know-how, addressing conflicts, dealing with the **Solicitors Regulation Authority** (**SRA**), which regulates the profession, and so on. Possibly the most important areas are client-focused, because without clients you have no work and without work you have no business. So it's no longer enough to be a technically proficient lawyer.

Before 1984 law firms in the UK weren't even allowed to talk to the press let alone market themselves (this was banned by the Law Society as 'touting'). Instead they were meant to garner client followings through personal reputation and standing.

Now of course a whole industry has grown up around **business development** (**BD**) for law firms, involving strategy consultants, PRs, advertising agencies, BD experts, networking trainers and pitching coaches plus a fully-fledged legal press comprising daily online bulletins, weekly newspapers, monthly magazines and annual directories telling clients which firms are the best at what and how much their partners earn. People can pursue entire careers working in the BD functions of law firms or in the legal press.

This has given clients, especially those with in-house legal departments staffed by lawyers who trained with the large firms, the information they need to drive hard bargains with their law firms. Law firms for their part have had to learn how to talk to clients about what they want and the price they are prepared to pay for it. Nowadays, partners who fail to win new business or to deliver adequate profitability are much more likely to be demoted (have their earnings – known as 'drawings' – reduced) or even kicked out altogether. Partners with strong client followings are able to jump ship at will and join other firms that promise to pay them more.

Law firms are now properly managed businesses with strategies, **CRM** (**client relationship management**) programmes, BD campaigns, USPs and so on. They have merged with each other and become bigger while the smaller ones have begun to disappear, a trend likely to continue if supermarkets and others offer commoditised legal services – a trend known as 'Tesco law'.

Large firms are regularly asked by companies and banks to **pitch for business**, that is, the prospective client will issue as many as a dozen firms with an **invitation to tender** (**ITT**) or **request for particulars** (**RFP**) – the two mean the same thing – then will use the firms' submissions to produce a short list of 3-4, then interview them and pick the winner. This can be for a particular job or to join the client's **panel of law firms** (the group of selected law firms it's prepared to use). Once a firm is on a panel it still has to fight to win each job – generally, by trying to submit the lowest quote. If it fails to do so often enough, it won't get much work from the client and will in due course be kicked off the panel and replaced by a keener firm.

Pricing

Traditionally solicitors charged by **time spent** on a client matter. But clients want **fixed fees** these days and the most sophisticated law firms keep a close check on how their lawyers are actually doing the work in order to keep within fixed fee quotes. From this firms can spot process improvements. By doing a particular type of work more efficiently, it allows a law firm to pitch for it at a lower price than others that aren't as efficient or which have to build in a bigger cushion for contingencies because they haven't done this sort of analysis.

So some firms are cornering the market in certain types of work and are conducting sophisticated discussions with clients about **pricing**.

The Six Pillars Of Pricing

Through working as a consultant advising in-house legal functions and law firms on pricing, I have identified six concerns that I believe clients have on their minds when they ask lawyers about fees. I've labelled them the **six pillars of pricing**.

1. How Much Will It Cost?

I know it sounds ridiculous but for a long time solicitors wouldn't even tell a client this (now they have to or, at least, the basis on which they are going to charge). There'd be a large insucking of breath over teeth, the way a mechanic or plumber does when they're about to tell you that whatever is wrong is going to cost a lot of money. But you still want to know how much. Clients are the same. They too need to know, whether they are an individual private client or a corporate. Private clients have budgets. Corporates have quarterly financial reporting. Each has to have an idea of what big items of expenditure they have coming up (which is why clients also like to be billed regularly and on time, something lawyers have been poor at grasping). You still get litigators who will shrug and say 'how long is a piece of string?' meaning that you can't predict how long a dispute will take to settle or come to court (or indeed which of the two it will do) so therefore you can't give a client an accurate estimate of cost. Clients don't find this helpful. Nowadays they want a fixed price, not just an hourly rate. An hourly rate on its own tells them nothing about how long (and so therefore how many hours at that rate) a job will take (and therefore cost). Even in litigation you can chunk a job, breaking it down into sections many of which you can attach a fixed price to.

2. Is That The Market Rate?

Clients also want to know whether your proposed charge is the market rate: if they were to shop around, would other lawyers quote roughly the same price? Some lawyers will low ball (quote a deliberately low price to win the work) because, for instance, they may be trying to win market share in that type of work. Which is fine. But clients are increasingly suspicious of lawyers who offer immediate discounts from their hourly rate (it makes the rate look artificially high if an immediate discount is offered). And firms that offer unrealistically low prices may end up cutting corners.

3. How Much Does This Matter To Me?

This is a factor that lawyers are poor at exploiting. From the lawyer's point of view, the work may be run-of-the-mill. One job is like another if they concern similar issues and areas of law. But for the client it may be especially important. It may be a divorce or M&A deal which they can expect to encounter (with luck) only rarely in their lives. Unlike 2 above which is an objective assessment of cost, this is subjective and will differ from client to client. If it matters a lot to the client to get the work done, they will pay more for it.

4. Have You Done This Sort Of Work Before?

This is where pricing is a proxy for track record. If a lawyer says he or she has done this type of work before, then the proof is in their ability to price it accurately. You'd be astonished the number of times a lawyer will pitch to the client, explaining just how many similar jobs the lawyer or his firm has done before, then be completely unable to come up with a precise price. If you can't price something tightly and you have to factor in a lot of headroom for contingencies, then the client is going to wonder whether you really know what you're talking about. Firms that have a more accurate assessment of price (by reviewing past transactions and seeing where the bottlenecks and costs arose) will be able to calibrate a keener quote with less headroom and so win the work. This becomes self-reinforcing: the more jobs they do, the keener the price, the greater their market share.

5.   How Much Of Your Inefficiency Am I Paying For?

A lot of clients are in-house lawyers who grew up as junior lawyers in firms and are now working in a company or bank's legal department. They're savvy. They know how lawyers and firms work, the inbuilt inefficiencies, the way junior lawyers learn on the job, how much of their work is actually useful and how much is just for their own education. Clients don't want to pay for junior lawyers who don't add value or for a slow lawyer's inefficiency or a lack of project management or process that leads to the wheel being reinvented all the time.

6.   Will You Go That Extra Mile?

This, like 3 above, is an area where lawyers miss a trick. If a client really likes you and trusts you to pull out all the stops and so wants to use you and nobody else, then this makes you more valuable to the client and you should charge appropriately highly. Instead most lawyers are so pleased to be loved that they charge clients less rather than more for being reliant on them. Equally, if a client thinks you're good and tells someone else they really should use you, then you can charge the new client more because they will be that much keener to act on that recommendation (which in turn helps you maintain the old rate for the existing client). However, most lawyers are so grateful to be recommended at all that they charge the new client less – and how does that make the client who recommended you feel if they recommended you and now the new client is paying less than them?

OK, these six pillars of pricing are a bit more advanced than putting a price on a tin of baked beans. But the principle is the same. Clients want to know how much something will cost before they buy it, and what they will get when they open the tin (no slugs or caterpillars, right?). And they will shop around to get the cheapest rate, unless you can persuade them that you are offering better **value for money** (**VFM**) or can differentiate your offering through brand or quality.

The Rules Of Profitability

Of course, it helps to know how law firms make money in the first place. **Stephen Mayson** answered this by devising the **RULES of profitability** – a model that identifies the financial levers in a law firm that affect its profitability.

R = Realised Rate

In the old days lawyers used to charge clients by 'weighing the file'. This isn't quite as dumb as it sounds. It's short-hand for saying that they would pick up the file and consider how much work it represented (how heavy it was), how complex that work and how important to the client, the importance of the client to the firm, and so on. This was an opaque process: alchemy rather than science. Over time clients wanted more clarity on the question of fees and how law firms fixed them. So the Law Society (since superseded by the SRA as the regulator) laid down seven factors that law firms should take into account. The overriding one (at least as interpreted by lawyers) was time: how much time a lawyer spends working on a file. There are other factors too: how complex the matter is, how much paperwork is involved, how much application of real expertise and so on.

But over time these all got boiled down to, well, time: how much a lawyer has on the clock. This was partly because commercial clients – big businesses with lawyers working in-house – would ask law firms for a print-out of the time recording records to verify the bill. So it all came down to time.

What's wrong with this? Everything. It rewards inefficiency: the lawyer who takes twice as long bills twice as much. It fails to give the client any certainty as to how much a piece of work is likely to cost. And it allows lawyers to live in an unreal world where they do the work, take as long as they like, bill the client and the client pays (I said a lot of this in an article I wrote for one of the solicitors' magazines and, unbelievably, it got quoted in Parliament. It must have been a slow day).

More and more clients are demanding fixed fees. This is a good thing. It forces lawyers to become more efficient, to adopt systematic processes for getting work done and to keep improving those processes.

Now in practice lawyers still use time recording at least as an internal measure. They start off with a notional hourly rate (aka **headline rate**) which tends to be higher the more senior a lawyer is to reflect his or her greater experience and expertise. But often the lawyer will offer a **discount** from this rate, for instance to reward the client for giving the firm a stream of work (this is called a **volume discount**). So this eats into the amount the firm will charge the client for the work.

Then a lawyer may fail to record all the time they spend on a matter (they may forget, or decide that they spent too long on a piece of work). This is called **moral editing**. It eats into the profitability of a piece of work because it means the firm is failing to capture part of the cost of doing the work. Then when the lawyer comes to bill the client the lawyer may **write down** (that is, reduce) the amount of recorded time to be charged. And when the client gets the bill they may refuse to pay part or all of it so that unpaid portion will be **written off** as time unrecovered.

The effect of all of this is that a lawyer with a charge-out rate of say £100 an hour (in the City a partner's rate will be many times this) who spends 30 hours on a job, may offer a 20% discount, record only 25 hours, decide that £2,000 (£80 x 25) is too much, bill £1,800 and be paid £1,500. This means that the lawyer's **realised rate** is in fact £50 an hour (£1,500 = 30 hours x £50) instead of the full £100 if he or she had charged the proper cost, which in this case would have been £3,000. Hence Mayson's emphasis on *realised* rate.

U = Utilisation

It means how busy the lawyers in a law firm are. If **utilisation** is 80% and a firm expects its lawyers to record 10 hours of **chargeable time** (chargeable = which clients can be charged for) a day, then they will only be recording eight hours of chargeable time. This will be because they don't have enough work to fill the other two hours. This means the partners need to go out and get more work from clients.

In some of the big City firms there may be too much work. Utilisation can often exceed 100%, with lawyers working into the evening, overnight and at weekends on a transaction. This is good for the law firm – the extra time charged over and above 100% utilisation (in this example, anything over 10 hours a day) is pure profit because lawyers don't get paid overtime. But it's not sustainable: lawyers get tired, they make mistakes, get fed up and may eventually leave. Most firms average about 90% utilisation. Don't forget that not all the time a lawyer spends in an office is chargeable. Lawyers do a lot of other things: business development; training younger lawyers; interviewing new recruits; appraising current staff; developing strategies; management and administration; and so on – none of these are chargeable.

As a rough rule of thumb most lawyers spend twice as long in the office as they clock up in chargeable time. So my example of 10 hours is too high. You'd need to spend a lot longer than that in the office, unless – as happens in big firms – you are working all day, every day on one big deal or case, when it is easier to clock up as chargeable time close to the actual time you're spending in the office.

L = Leverage

Leverage, which is also known as **gearing**, is the ratio of partners to other fee-earners. At first blush, the more fee-earners you have per partner the more money you should make because you have more employees (fee-earners) generating profit for the employer (partner). In practice – and Stephen Mayson's work shows this – whether you do or not depends on whether the firm attracts the sort of work that can be delegated down sufficiently to keep fee-earners profitably busy. For more on this see 'What law firms need partners to do' below, which is also based on Stephen Mayson's work. On the whole, the biggest and most profitable firms tend to have higher leverage than smaller firms (you do get small firms that have more partners than fee-earners and which are highly profitable, but that's because the individual partners have high realised rates and work long hours).

This throws up an interesting side-effect: every time a firm promotes a fee-earner to partnership it has to recruit more fee-earners to maintain its leverage, if that's what its profitability is premised on. In the 1980s and 1990s this led the biggest firms to get bigger still as they promoted fee-earners to partnership and recruited more fee-earners to take their place (and if your leverage is 5:1 that means that every time you promote someone to partnership you need to recruit another five fee-earners). All these newcomers would themselves have partnership aspirations which have to be managed.

E = Expenses

Expenses is easier to grasp. It means simply that you have to keep your outgoings in check and the more you do so, the higher your profitability. There is just one snag. Traditionally law firms' highest costs are premises and people. Premises means office space. This is pretty inflexible: law firms enter into business tenancies of several years for their premises and these costs are not easily reduced unless the landlord is prepared to renegotiate (which, in the main, commercial landlords aren't prepared to do). So if you can't reduce your premises costs you have to look to reducing headcount.

But people are hard to get rid of and usually cost money to do so; besides, large firms find that if they get rid of younger lawyers, say in response to a recession, then several years later they have a gap in expertise at the level that those junior lawyers would now have filled. So firms then have to recruit in the market which is always expensive and of more variable quality than training your own junior lawyers.

So if premises and people are a firm's biggest slugs of expenditure (each accounting for as much as 30-40%) what about the rest? The rest tend to be **variable costs** – that is, they go up and down (vary) depending on how busy the firm is: the busier it is the higher these are. But they are pretty small beer by comparison: phones, electricity, paper and stationery, postage, that sort of thing.

S = Speed

Speed is about how quickly a firm gets paid for the work it has done. Let's say I set up as a sole practitioner today and I get a client and start work on the matter. It takes three months to complete and I bill on completion. It takes four weeks for the client to pay me. That means I've waited four months to get any cash in. But over that period I've had to pay outgoings – rent and rates, utilities, secretary's salary, quite apart from drawing any money myself to live on. This 'gap' between paying money out and getting money in is a **cash flow** gap and is bridged by something called **working capital**. I find this term misleading because capital is something I associate with a one-off payment for something substantial – a capital payment to buy a car for instance. But working capital is the money I need to stay in business – to allow me to pay my bills while waiting to be paid myself.

There are two sources of working capital: (1) I can borrow it from the bank; (2) I can inject my own money into the business. Either way there's a cost: interest I pay to the bank; or the investment return I would have got from investing my money elsewhere. Either cost reduces the overall profitability (return to me) of the work.

Firms try very hard to reduce this gap between doing the work and getting paid. They do this through a number of ways, for example: getting **paid on account** (getting some money upfront when a client is taken on); and **interim billing** (billing regularly during the course of a matter for the work done, rather than at the end). In these ways they reduce their **work-in-progress** (**WIP**) that is, work that has been done but not billed, and their **debtors**, that is, amounts owing from clients for work that has been billed but not paid.

But this is a one-off benefit: if you get your work-in-progress down and your debtors in hand, you get an immediate cash boost that improves your profitability by reducing your working capital requirement. But you then have to be rigorous in enforcing this degree of WIP and debtor management. If WIP and debtors increase, then your working capital requirement increases and your profitability is reduced.

So those are Stephen Mayson's RULES of profitability. He also came up with another wonderfully insightful model which identified what a law firm needs its partners to do.

What Law Firms Need Partners To Do

Most partners in law firms believe – or they did until Stephen Mayson came along – that their job was fee-earning. He showed them by an arithmetic model that it isn't. He showed that if you want to earn a lot of money as a lawyer you can't do it on your own, because you'd have to work more hours than there are in a day and on top of that you'd have to go out and get clients, manage a secretary, do all the billing and admin and so on. And you'd be exposed to risks such as illness, lack of clients and your expertise no longer being required in the market.

But if you hire associates to work for you, whatever they earn for you over and above what they cost (in salary and overhead) is profit that you keep. This is the economics of big law firms: partners earn a lot because of the associates who may earn for the firm 2-3 times what they cost. That profit goes to the partners as owners of the business.

But, and this is the point, what Mayson's model goes on to show is that for this to happen partners have to do a lot of things: winning clients and business; keeping clients happy; fronting up the work to them; keeping associates fully utilised; managing the associates by delegating the work to them and supervising how it's done; managing associates' expectations of partnership; and so on. In fact the one thing a partner shouldn't do in these circumstances is any actual fee-earning work.

Now this is a counsel of perfection: all partners need to do some fee-earning work to keep their hand in (besides, supervising associates on a matter is itself work that is chargeable to that matter); but it's only a small component of what the day job should be. Mayson may have painted an extreme picture to make a point.

But the point is that partners need to do more of everything else and less of the actual fee-earning. And partners often don't like this message because it takes them out of their comfort zone which is just doing the law. Which is why Mayson's model is such a shock to the system.

How Law Is Subject To Commoditisation

Another model – this time from **David Maister**, another law firm management guru – has proved influential in law firm management. It's known as the **3Es**. Maister says that all areas of legal expertise start out as **Expertise** (that is, rocket science) then over time become a matter of **Experience** (you can do it if you've done one before) and finally end up as **Efficiency** work (the legal content is low and the work is more a matter of process).

Three types of work that have become Efficiency are: residential conveyancing; debt collection; and bond issuance. Residential conveyancing used to be the staple of high street practice. Solicitors charged a lot for it. Now it's done by licensed conveyancers and costs a couple of hundred quid. With the switch to registered title (see Chapter 6) the whole idea behind residential conveyancing is that it should be automatic: people see a house and they should be able to buy it.

So nowadays the most successful residential conveyancing businesses have automated the process. They're known as conveyancing 'factories' and the work's all done by low-level operatives using drop-down menus generating standard-form letters and documents.

Debt collection and bond issuance have gone the way of residential conveyancing. Debt collection is now a fully-automated business. Indeed there's a firm in the north-west of England that consists of one solicitor and about fifty staff which is one of the most profitable debt collection firms around. And why not? If you can provide an efficient, automated service at a price that customers are happy to pay and you can make a lot of money doing so, then good luck to you.

I mention bond issuance because it's at the other end of the spectrum. Residential conveyancing and debt collection are examples of high street practice. But bond issuance is the preserve of the biggest international law firms in the City of London. A bond is a kind of corporate IOU. Companies and governments issue them to raise money (loans) in the international capital markets. Investment banks get involved since they distribute these bonds to investors and underwrite these issues, that is, they effectively guarantee to the issuer that it will still raise the money it needs even if the bonds it issues aren't bought.

Now the point is this: this all sounds pretty complex stuff involving huge amounts of money. Certainly in the 1970s when bond issues in London became popular, law firms could charge £50,000 a pop. Now it's more like a tenth of that because all of the necessary documentation has become so standardised that it isn't much more than pressing a button and churning out tried-and-tested legal agreements.

So Maister's point is that almost all areas of legal practice are subject to commoditisation over time.

Just as an aside, Maister's 3Es plug directly into Mayson's RULES (see above) in relation to Leverage. Expertise areas of practice don't lend themselves to much leverage: you tend to need a partner doing the bulk of the work with maybe one associate. Experience is different: maybe one partner to three associates. Efficiency can be as leveraged as you like: one solicitor to fifty non-legal staff (although that's at the extreme end). You can begin to see how that solicitor doing debt collection in the north-west has been as profitable as he has.

Mayson has added a fourth E to Maister's 3Es. It stands for **Extinction**. And that's what happens to lawyers and law firms who fail to grasp this.

However you look at it, being a successful lawyer, whether you're a partner in one of the largest law firms in the world or running a small high street practice or any and all points in between, is tough. It is a tough job. Just being on top of the law is intellectually challenging. But these days you have to develop skills in so many other different areas as well, as we've seen. All of this requires hard work and long hours. Being an in-house lawyer is no easier, working in the legal department of a company or bank. It too is a demanding job that requires long hours.

So even if the best-paid lawyers in this country – solicitors in the largest law firms and QCs at the Bar – earn a lot of money, it isn't easy and, basically, the more you earn the less time you have to spend it. So, if you want to become a lawyer just to earn a lot of money, my advice is: don't. There are easier ways of earning more.

Two Tales From Different Ends Of The Profession

By contrast to big firms and top QCs, one of my favourite clients when I was a consultant was a six-partner firm in an up-market town in the home counties. It was a highly prestigious local firm offering the full range of legal services that the wealthy local populace might need. The firm was over a hundred years old and a couple of the partners had come from large London firms. They had about 15 lawyers and a further 30 other staff. They were well managed. And they all worked really hard. And yet they didn't seem – at least to my mind – to be making all that much money for the effort they were putting in, the quality of their work and clients, and the business risks the six partners were shouldering.

So they consulted a company doctor (a financial turnaround specialist who can pinpoint where a business could improve financially). He did some analysis and came to present his findings at a **partnership retreat** (when a law firm's partners go away for a weekend to discuss the firm's strategy, business and management – also known as an **offsite**) which I was facilitating for them.

He showed them the figures of two law firms, similar in practice to them. One was their size with their level of mediocre profitability. They guessed correctly that this firm was in fact them. But the other was a much smaller firm – just six lawyers plus their secretaries. This firm was making lots of money. He said it was a local firm but he wouldn't reveal its name.

'Which one do you want to be?' he asked them.

The second one, of course, they answered. The one with the six lawyers and their secretaries and nobody else.

'So which firm is it?' he asked.

They racked their brains. They couldn't think which other firm local to them it could be.

'Oh, come on, you must know!' he exhorted them. 'All of you know them.'

No dice. They had no idea.

'It's you,' he revealed, 'but just the six of you in this room and your secretaries, without the rest.'

They were amazed. In other words their profitability was being eaten up by the number of employees they had – lawyers and support staff – who were enjoying well paid jobs at the partners' expense. They had the leverage but weren't using it properly. They weren't keeping their staff properly utilised.

By contrast, one of the consultancy projects I worked on for a top law firm was helping it pinpoint what qualities enabled lawyers to become successful partners in the firm – after all, promotion to partnership, you will have gathered, is the goal of associates in a big law firm: it's the reason why they work all hours, to become partners with all of the money and prestige that follow.

Most big firms operate an 'up-or-out' policy: you either make partner by your mid-thirties or you leave. Some firms allow lawyers who don't make partner to stay, for instance remaining as senior associates or becoming 'of counsel' and this suits some people. But for the truly ambitious, becoming a partner is what it's all about because it sets you on a prestigious and lucrative career path.

So I talked to lawyers who'd just been made partners to find out from them what it took. One such was a recently-promoted banking partner. I congratulated her on her appointment. After all, you don't get promoted in a firm like this particular one unless you are extremely bright, extraordinarily hard working, can manage others and are great with clients.

'This must be the goal of everything you set out to achieve,' I said.

She agreed, but added: 'As a senior associate I was running two or three matters. If a junior did some work on one and I wasn't happy with it I could stay late and redo it – redraft the agreement or whatever. Now I'm responsible for about fourteen or fifteen matters at any one time. I don't have time to check what's happening on all of them let alone do any remedial work. All I can do is go round kicking the tyres. And if I'm in the office and not out at a client's, I get senior associates on matters that aren't mine coming to me with questions because their own partners are out. And these questions are by definition difficult ones, otherwise why else would they come to me?'

Then she laughed, meaning that the same strength of mind that had got her a partnership would see her through this next set of challenges. The firm knew she'd make it. It's why they had picked her. The partners she had worked for on her way up had spotted she was a star in the making.

Stars In The Making

This is just one of the ways in which law firms can be quite strange places to work. There is very little apparent hierarchy. Lawyers are trainees, associates or partners. Some firms insert intermediate stages like managing associate or, as mentioned earlier, senior associate, but essentially that's it: you're a trainee or a qualified lawyer (solicitor) or a partner.

But beneath this apparently flat structure there are lots of feudal hierarchies. I was doing some work in one large firm and managed to offend a very powerful partner. I went to another partner (also a senior partner) who was my mentor on the project and confessed all. 'Don't worry,' my **mentor** said to me, 'I'll have a word with him. He used to be my trainee.' What this means is that as lawyers grow up in a firm they remain beholden to their very first mentors and those relationships never change.

However, compared to many organisations, the politics in law firms is generally mild: lawyers are intelligent people who enjoy what they do (law) so organisational politics is rarely ingrained.

Another partner I know came to give a talk to some newly qualifieds. They had just finished their training contracts as trainees and were becoming fully qualified solicitors.

I had first met him when he was just coming up to partnership. He attended a five-day residential training programme that the firm held at a business school in order to get its senior associates teed up to become partners. I was one of the external faculty. He spent the whole week with one leg dangling over the arm of his chair, slouching in a kind of uninvolved way.

But I could tell from the one or two things that he said that it was all going in. He was a partner in the making (with some you can just tell; with others, they need these sorts of training programmes to bring the best out of them and ensure they don't slip through the net). In fact within a year he was rated by one of the legal publications as one of the top one hundred most influential lawyers in the UK. He was still only in his early thirties.

I heard conflicting stories about him. His team loved him; his team hated him. He wasn't a very good lawyer; he came up with innovative solutions. He worked incredibly hard; he left his team working on deals overnight while he went home. Whether any of this was true or not was beside the point. The point was that he was a legend. And amongst the gossip and speculation one thing was clear: clients loved him.

Anyway, apart from still being involved in the five-day residential programme, I was also running a one-day programme at that same firm for the trainee solicitors who were just qualifying and so were just setting out on their careers. So that's when I asked him if he would come and talk to them for half-an-hour before lunch. I knew he'd be inspirational. I also knew he'd say no. He was far too busy to bother with a roomful of kids.

But he surprised me. He said yes. We agreed the date and the time: 12 noon, a half-hour slot before lunch.

On the day in question it was five past twelve and he was nowhere to be seen. Of course he might not show up. That was the risk you ran in asking such a successful young partner. He would have clients baying for him and his team demanding his support whenever one of his deals became problematic. It was only to be expected that he'd relegate this to the bottom of the list.

I was just giving up hope, and trying to think of something to keep 40 young and impatient lawyers occupied to fill the gap till lunch, when the door flew open and in he came, immaculately turned out.

He was electrifying.

'I'm really sorry I'm late,' he began. 'I've just had six banks on the phone demanding a legal opinion off us which we need to give to enable them to fund a deal. I've promised they'll have it in half-an-hour. But this is important to me. You are the future of this firm and talking to you is a privilege for me.'

He paused dramatically.

'And I know what you're all thinking.'

The room was already dead silent but as soon as he said that I felt everyone straighten up and crane forward, on the edge of their seats. He had their undivided attention. How could he know what they were all thinking?

'What you're thinking is: how can I get to be where he is.' In other words, how could they become partners like him too.

It was brilliant and it was true. That firm was the sort of place where you don't muck about. You go there to work like stink and become a partner. And what you want to become is not just any old partner. You want to become a star, like him.

And then he did a little dance.

He waved one arm snake-like up by his shoulder. 'You've got to be good to your secretary.' Then he pivoted and almost squatted down. 'And be nice to the partner.' Then he turned and levelled his arm out. 'And be liked by the clients.' And so it went on.

With the little dance he showed them who they had to impress and who they had to keep happy.

Then he turned to face them and said: 'Which is it better to be: rushing round, looking busy, making a lot of noise? Or calm, getting things done quietly and purposefully?' Again he paused. Then he answered his own question. 'The latter, of course. Think of it from the partners' point of view: they want people who look as if they are in control, not as if they're in a panic all day.' Yet most lawyers did the opposite, thinking it looked impressive and made them look important.

He concluded by saying: 'In a place like this you can make your own rules. I have a young family so I make sure I see them at the beginning or end of the day. Some days I'm in by seven and leave at four. Other days I come in at ten and work till midnight. And when I leave I don't care who knows. And I don't leave my jacket on the back of the chair' – he was referring to the common practice in City law firms of trying to make it look as if you are still in the office by leaving your jacket there, because in all major firms there is a culture of working all hours. Again, most lawyers did the opposite and were slaves to the firm's culture. He wasn't. Yet he'd succeeded.

And with that he looked at his watch and said: 'Must dash. Can't keep our clients waiting.'

And he was gone. In a puff of smoke. Like the White Rabbit.

The room was stunned. It had been a bravura performance.

So how do you start, if you want to be like him?

Types Of Lawyer

The two most obvious routes to becoming a lawyer at all are as a solicitor or a barrister.

At the time of writing, the two most popular ways of becoming a **solicitor** are:

- Do a law degree (2 or 3 years) followed by the legal practice course (1 year or less) then a training contract at a law firm or legal department (2 years) after which you automatically qualify as a solicitor = 6 years or

- Do any degree (non-law) then a graduate diploma in law (1 year) then the legal practice course (LPC) as above and the training contract as above = 7 years. If you're reading this and thinking that sounds a long way off, all it really means is you study for a year or two after uni. The rest you do by learning on the job.

To become a **barrister** you follow either route as above but do the Bar Professional Training Course (BPTC) instead of the LPC, followed by pupillage at a barristers' chambers instead of a training contract at a law firm.

Another popular route, especially for those who come to law late, and who are qualifying while they are in full-time employment, is by becoming a **legal executive**. To do this you have to have passed the exams set by CILEx (the Chartered Institute of Legal Executives). Legal executives can't do everything a solicitor can (for instance, they can't appear in court) and, if they work in a law firm, need to be supervised by a solicitor. It isn't a quick route – it can take five years or more, through part-time and evening study. But once you have CILEx you can convert to being a solicitor. I used to teach the CILEx programme at my local further education college and I think it's an excellent, practical course – in many respects every bit as good as a law degree.

However, you can do some types of legal work without being fully qualified. For example, **paralegals** tend to be young professionals who want to become lawyers but haven't actually qualified as a barrister or solicitor. Technically they aren't therefore lawyers but have often done the LPC or BPTC without being able to obtain a training contract or pupillage. So they get jobs with the larger law firms to do some of the more routine administrative work such as research or collating the documentation required in big transactions and court cases. Some may remain paralegals. Others hope to get a training contract later, with the firm in which they are working or in another firm. Related to this is the idea behind legal apprenticeships, to enable school leavers without a degree to get into law.

Then there are **licensed conveyancers** who are only allowed to do property work, principally buying and selling residential property (flats and houses).

People with a science background often choose to become **patent attorneys** instead of solicitors or barristers. A patent attorney is not a lawyer but is equally as qualified. A lot of the work they do is legal in nature. Essentially a patent attorney files patents which are used to protect inventions. Whether or not an invention or improvement in an existing process or product merits a patent is a highly technical issue. Patent attorneys help inventors and big businesses that rely on patents (everything from drinks to drugs and industrial processes) to file patents, protect them against infringements and license them for commercial exploitation. **Trademark agents** are similar but specialise in trademarks (logos and brands).

Patents, trademarks and copyright (you'll see at the front of this book that it is copyrighted) together form, as I've mentioned, intellectual property (the protection and exploitation of products of the mind – such as art, music, books, films, brands, etc) in which solicitors, barristers, patent attorneys and trademark agents specialise. It is harder, in my opinion, to become a patent attorney than a solicitor or barrister. The best ones do a science degree, followed by a succession of exams laid down by the CIPA (The Chartered Institute of Patent Attorneys) which take several years and have a high failure rate.

In addition, there are some very odd corners of legal qualification, such as **notaries** and **scriveners** whose role is really about the authentication of legal documents. This mattered in the past when legal documents were hand-written on parchment and needed to be authenticated. But nowadays with technology and electronic communication these roles are fading in importance. In civil law countries you still need a notary to validate a land transfer, for instance.

Many lawyers of all types choose to work in the legal departments of companies, banks and central and local government as well as for third-sector organisations (such as charities). They are known as **in-house lawyers**. Thirty years ago when I was starting out this was regarded as very much a second-rate option. The best lawyers joined the top City law firms and rose through the ranks to become partners. No one in their right mind would go in-house to do a sort of company secretarial job. How times have changed. Some of the most interesting jobs in the law involve acting as **general counsel** (a US term meaning the top lawyer in a company).

These are highly demanding roles, often involving advising the board of a big public company, and are well rewarded. They can lead on to top corporate positions as CEOs of major companies. And they involve management – often of hundreds of lawyers. These in-house 'heads of legal' are law firms' most important clients because they decide what work to keep in-house and what to farm out to external firms and – crucially – what they are prepared to pay those firms to do that work. Best of all, you can start off in private practice (that is, working for a law firm), then move in-house, then move back out again and become a partner in a firm, because your experience as an in-house lawyer (seeing things from a client's perspective) is hugely valuable to law firms.

The other type of in-house function is working in the public sector, as a lawyer in central government or for a local authority. These, too, have become highly regarded, well-paid and interesting jobs. In central government you can work for TSol (Treasury Solicitors) advising the government or as a parliamentary draftsman (crafting legislation – remember Sir Benjamin Cherry who drafted that suite of brilliant legislation in 1925?). In local government some local authorities have turned their legal departments into profit centres, doing work for other authorities as well.

Then there is the third sector, working in-house for charities and NGOs (non-governmental organisations), for example for educational bodies, trade associations, voluntary organisations, faith groups and social enterprises. So the sky really is the limit.

Business Services And Support Staff

One other point. As law firms have got bigger they've needed more and more non-legal staff in roles every bit as professional as those of the lawyers themselves. So, for example, in the largest law firms you get people in finance, technology, human resources, facilities management, business development, corporate communications, training, research, libraries and knowledge management (capturing lawyers' know-how in documents and making that know-how and those documents available to others). These functions are known collectively as **business services** or **support staff**.

This means that major law firms are now viable places to pursue a career even if you aren't, or don't want to remain, a lawyer. If you are a lawyer, better still, because you understand what lawyers do and what they are like. In my case it's enabled me to undertake roles in business development, training and knowledge management in large law firms.

Types Of Law Firm

So far I've been talking about larger law firms. Here I want to cover all types of firm:

Sole practitioners / sole principals are solicitors who work on their own (sole practitioner) or as the only partner (sole principal) with assistant solicitors (aka associates). The work they tend to do includes residential conveyancing, wills and probate, matrimonial and personal injury.

Legal aid firms are firms that gain the bulk of their income from doing legal work paid for by the government's legal aid scheme. The work they do includes criminal, immigration and human rights law.

High street firms have two or more partners plus some assistants. They will do a combination of residential conveyancing, wills and probate, matrimonial and child custody, personal injury, employment (for employees), commercial contracts for small businesses, and the buying and selling of small businesses. Some high street firms have developed high volume practices in residential conveyancing (often with an estate agency attached), remortgaging and debt collection. Some do litigation in areas such as personal injury and employment.

Medium sized firms tend to be ten-plus partners strong. They will do all of the work that high street firms do but also more commercial work for small and medium sized owner-managed businesses including commercial property, employment and pensions (for employers) and even intellectual property and tax. Some have national reputations, for instance for medical negligence. Some have financial services businesses serving wealthy personal clients.

Regional firms are firms with several offices in one part of the country. They do everything medium sized firms do but with more emphasis on commercial clients and less on personal clients. They tend to serve large commercial clients and do (some) work for public companies, as well as serving large privately-owned companies, their directors and owners, and local public bodies (local authorities, schools and so on). They also have litigation practices covering dispute resolution in commercial, employment and landlord & tenant.

National firms are firms with offices in the principal cities around the country. They focus on corporate and commercial clients (including public bodies) rather than personal clients. Principal areas of practice include: corporate, commercial, banking and finance, employment and pensions, tax, commercial property, planning, environment, intellectual property, media and technology, trusts, charities and education. They have comprehensive litigation expertise in these areas too.

City law firms focus principally on (1) equity finance (companies floating on the London Stock Exchange) and M&A (mergers and acquisitions – public companies taking each other over) and (2) debt finance which comprises bank lending (banking) and bond issuance and underwriting (capital markets – a term that can also include equity finance where a share issue is made internationally).

These firms tend to have a whole range of other expertise too. Corporate work requires a tax capability as well as competition law (in case a merger resulting from a takeover is considered market dominant under EU law) – the latter explaining why they usually have a Brussels office. Company acquisitions require due diligence (vetting the target in all sorts of areas) so the full range of legal expertise is required in, for instance, employment and pensions, intellectual property, real estate, planning and environmental, and so on.

On the banking side, these firms will have expertise in all sorts of banking-related areas such as asset finance, trade finance and project finance. They may also do property finance which, with real estate work for corporates, means that some firms have strong commercial property practices serving institutional investors that own large commercial property and retail developments. They may also have strong financial services and funds practices, advising investment funds and private equity funds.

Some firms also have strong litigation practices in the contentious aspects of all of their non-contentious practices. Some of the smaller City law firms have retained (and developed their) private client practices, acting for high-net-worth individuals (as the very rich are called).

International law firms – the biggest City law firms are very international because English law is used as a governing law in transactions all over the world. With so much of their work and clients in other countries, the biggest City law firms are amongst the largest in the world with offices in all of the major jurisdictions. Most of the largest are banking and capital markets powerhouses (known as the **magic circle**), serving big banks globally. Others may have strengths in corporate and commercial law, serving multinational companies around the world.

Still others may be smaller and more niche, for instance specialising in shipping and international trade, with expertise in related areas such as commodities, insurance and reinsurance, oil, gas and energy, transportation law generally and ship and aircraft finance.

London is a favoured location for international litigation. Firms that have a litigation capability will also have strong international arbitration practices which centre on Paris.

So that's the work of everyday lawyers: law from the bottom up. Now – finally – let's look at law from the top down: the English Legal System.

CHAPTER 10

JUDGES MAKING LAW: THE ENGLISH LEGAL SYSTEM

Constitutional law – administrative law – English Legal System (ELS) –
statutes – Acts of Parliament – green paper – white paper –
administrative actions – judicial review – mandamus – certiorari – habeas
corpus – Law Commission – courts of first instance – appealed – point of
fact – points of law – Court of Appeal – Supreme Court – county courts –
High Court – magistrates' courts – Crown Court – European Court of
Justice – European Court of Human Rights – Privy Council – precedents
– distinguish – law reports – common law system – Inns of Court –
English legal history – justice of the peace – ecclesiastical law – ratio
decidendi – dissenting judgment – minority judgment – obiter dictum

So far we've looked at the five pillars of law – criminal, tort, contract, equity and property – and at legal practice. This leaves just two topics to cover, possibly the most fundamental of all: how law gets made (this chapter); and how it relates to morality and societal norms – also known as the philosophy of law or jurisprudence (next chapter).

How law gets made is known to law students as 'Consti & Admin' which is short for:

- **Constitutional law** – basically the law that governs the law makers; and
- **Administrative law** – how law is administered, which includes the **English Legal System** (**ELS**), which is how the courts work.

Most law books and law courses do Consti & Admin first. I've never understood this. It can be such a dry subject that to start with it strikes me as the kiss of death. Who cares how the courts work and legislation is passed if you don't know what the law is or what lawyers do?

So I've left it till last on the basis that I hope you have now gained sufficient insight into, and (dare I say it if you've got this far?) interest in, the law to want to know about how it's made and applied: the meta-law (the law about law) that determines how law comes into existence, how it is interpreted and so on; and the court system that helps support and shape it.

1. How Law Is Made

Parliament enacts **statutes** (called **Acts of Parliament**). These are almost always introduced by government (since it alone has a majority to get legislation passed and to block anybody else's). Usually legislation is preceded by a **green paper** in which government sets out its approach (often soliciting views), then a **white paper** which is a more technical discussion document and forms the basis of the legislation.

Once an Act of Parliament has been laid before Parliament and passed, it has to be signed by the monarch and then comes into force on a specified date (the point at which it becomes the law of the land) for the courts to apply thereafter. There may be subsidiary bits of legislation – such as statutory instruments and orders – that bring new laws into force in stages.

The Poor Quality Of Statutory Drafting

If you're one of those who subscribes to the view that everything is going to the dogs, you're in good company. The judges think so too. They think the modern law they have to apply is badly written. And they don't seem to think things are poised to get better.

You'll remember that lawyers swoon at the clarity of the Law of Property Act 1925. By contrast the more recent Criminal Justice Act 2003 has come in for criticism on more than one occasion from Lord Justice Rose. In December 2005, sitting in the High Court, Rose LJ (LJ means Lord Justice – what judges in the top courts are called) laid into the 'deeply confusing provisions' of the CJA 2003 and said it would be tempting for judges, 'having shaken their heads in despair, to hold up their hands and say: the Holy Grail of rational interpretation is impossible to find. But it is not for us to desert our judicial duty, however lamentably others have legislated'. And he referred back to 'a time when elegance and clarity of thought and language were to be found in legislation as a matter of course rather than exception'. This was followed, a few months later in March 2006, by the same Rose LJ (this time in the Court of Appeal) complaining about CJA 2003's provisions, 'a considerable number of which are, at best, obscure and, at worst, impenetrable'.

This is strong stuff from a senior member of the judiciary in criticising the legislature, not least since part of Consti's purpose is to keep the executive (government), the legislature (law-making body) and the judiciary (body of judges who interpret the law) apart. If each of these is distinct and equal, there is a separation and balance of powers for the benefit of society and the individual. Or, to put it simply, the courts (judiciary), Parliament (legislature) and the government (executive) need to be, and be seen to be, separate. You don't want government telling the judges how to decide cases; nor ignoring the citizens' elected representative body (Parliament), for instance by abolishing it. You want each part to be open to scrutiny and held to account.

Constitutional Law – A Conundrum

The very first question I had to deal with as a law student at uni was whether Parliament can bind itself. In other words can the legislature (the law-making body) pass a law that restricts its ability to make law in the future? Can it say: this particular law we are enacting is binding on us for all future time and we cannot change it in the future?

The answer is: no; Parliament can always purport to bind itself but then the next day change its mind and ignore what it said yesterday. That way at any given moment it is **sovereign**. (That's still the theory – though it's taken some doing at times to maintain this idea of sovereignty in the face of what Denning called the 'tidal wave' of EU law.)

Administrative Law Examples

Government is itself subject to law through what are called **administrative actions**. Here are some examples. **Judicial review** is the action (court case) you can bring against government if you don't like what it's doing. What you have to show is that something the government has done is so unreasonable that no one (i.e. a minister) could have reasonably arrived at that decision. It's a pretty high threshold (i.e. difficult to establish), not least because the judiciary has always been reluctant to interfere in government decisions. **Mandamus** (loosely, 'show us') is an action you can bring when government seems to be doing nothing and is therefore in dereliction of a statutory duty to do something. **Certiorari** (pronounced 'sasha-rary' – as in Tipperary) is an action that requires government to do something specific that it so far hasn't but should have done.

The one administrative action you may have heard of is **habeas corpus** or, to give it its full name, the writ of habeas corpus (all of these actions are writs which is just the old name for 'claim'). Habeas corpus (literally: 'you have' the / a 'body') is used when someone is being held (indefinitely) without being brought to trial. For instance, if the Guantanamo Bay prisoners had been held in the UK, they would have been able to bring claims of habeas corpus requiring the state to try them in court or else release them.

Law Commission

If government is passing bad laws, as Rose LJ and others suggest, it's not for want of trying. There is, after all, the **Law Commission**. Created by statute (the snappily entitled Law Commission Act 1965), its job is to keep an eye on the law and make recommendations for the law's improvement. The only problem is that most of its suggestions are ignored by government, which is a shame because many of them are pretty sound. Perhaps the Law Commission should suggest its own abolition by proposing the repeal of the Law Commission Act 1965 – in the certain knowledge government will ignore it.

If this is how law is made, how is it applied?

2. How Law Is Applied

We already know how this happens: through the **courts of first instance**. These are the criminal and civil courts that first hear cases. Almost all cases are dealt with at that level. But a small fraction are **appealed**, either on a point of law or a point of fact. It is much harder to appeal on a **point of fact**: the appellate courts are very reluctant to go back over the evidence heard in a lower court just because one side said the factual evidence was incomplete or faulty in some way.

Points of law are different, but by their nature are far less common. Here the appellant (the party appealing) is saying that the inferior (lower) court got the law or procedure wrong. Cases that get as far as the **Court of Appeal** (CoA) or beyond often change the law by departing from precedent, which is why so many of the cases mentioned in this book are CoA or House of Lords cases (the **Supreme Court** has replaced the House of Lords).

The appeal system is a bit messy.

Civil cases go from **county courts** (or the magistrates' courts in respect of matrimonial) to the High Court, where appeals are heard before what are called the Divisional Courts of the **High Court**. So, for example, appeals of matrimonial cases from magistrates' courts will be heard by the Divisional Court of the Family Division of the High Court.

Criminal appeals go from **magistrates' courts** to the **Crown Court**. From the Crown Court they go to the CoA, although some criminal cases are appealed from the Crown Court to the Divisional Court of the Queen's Bench Division of the High Court rather than direct to the CoA.

When cases go up to the CoA, criminal cases go to the Criminal Division of the CoA and civil cases to the Civil Division. Both types then go to the Supreme Court.

You generally need leave to appeal from the High Court to go up to the CoA (appeals are allowed on law or fact) and leave of the CoA to go up to the Supreme Court (appeals on law only, or issues of general public importance).

The Impact Of Europe

That isn't the end of it. We saw earlier that the **European Court of Justice** can be asked to clarify points of EU law. For their part, human rights cases can be appealed to the **European Court of Human Rights**.

Indeed, Europe (and the separation of powers) is the reason why the Supreme Court has replaced the House of Lords. The House of Lords was both the UK's top court and also the second camera (= Latin for 'room' so 'in camera' = 'in private') of Parliament. In short, the judiciary and the legislature were not as separate as the EU would have liked. In theory any lord could actually sit as a judge in the court of the House of Lords (on occasion a non-lawyer peer might try to muscle in, but the lords who were there because they were professional judges elevated to the peerage for that reason would gently chuck him or her out).

So, to cut a long story short, the abolition of the House of Lords as a court and its replacement by the Supreme Court acknowledged this division between legislature and judiciary in line with EU principles. It was foreshadowed by the split in the Lord Chancellor (LC)'s role. The LC was previously in charge of the judges (the judiciary), was the Leader of the Lords (legislature) and, being a political appointee, was part of government (executive) – hence the need to split the role.

At the risk of confusing you further, there is also the **Privy Council**. It too is a kind of ultimate court but one that hears appeals from former commonwealth countries. Most noteworthy have been a succession of criminal cases from the Caribbean – essentially appeals against death sentences which are still imposed in some countries and which the Privy Council has tended to commute (reduce) to life imprisonment. I suspect that over time most former commonwealth countries will block this right of appeal as being anachronistic, however well-intentioned and morally right the Privy Council may appear to be.

Other Courts And Tribunals

You may be surprised to learn that in addition there used to be a whole load of other courts and tribunals too, covering everything from immigration to transport and rating valuations to gambling. Since 2010, these have all been combined into a generic First Tier Tribunal, from which appeals are made to the Upper Tribunal.

3.   How Cases Establish Precedents

So the law, having been enacted by Parliament, is then applied by the courts to cases, which requires the judges (who preside over the courts) to interpret these statutes. In doing this they may (inadvertently) make new law, although they tend to deny that they do so. Also, as you know, these cases establish **precedents** which are then followed by courts in future cases.

You might be surprised at the degree of flexibility this gives judges. After all, you might reasonably think that since statutes lay down the latest law and previous cases have precedential value there isn't much room for judicial discretion. But no two cases have identical facts and applying a single statute to lots of different circumstances is not an exact science by any means. So there is always an element of flexibility in applying what the law seems to say (and that's an act of interpretation in its own right – especially if modern-day statutes are as badly drafted as they appear to be) to the immediate facts before the court. Courts have various ways of wriggling out of previous precedents. The most common is to **distinguish** a case on its facts. This assumes you know what the previous cases are and say.

Law Reports

For cases to establish precedents, they must be recorded somehow. Court judgments get taken down and published in **law reports** which appear in different series. The most well-known are the All ER (the All England law reports) and the WLR (which stands for the Weekly Law Reports). These end up being leather-bound and filling whole walls of law libraries. There are series such as the QBD – Queen's Bench Division – that go back hundreds of years (KBD when a king's on the throne).

But here's an interesting thing that is a microcosm of the fundamental absurdity of a lot of English common law: (1) not all court decisions get written down (judgments in short, straightforward cases are given orally by the judge); (2) which cases get reported is down to the editors of the law reports; and (3) – which I think just about takes the biscuit – the law reports are all a matter of private enterprise. Apart from a period under James I, law reporting has never been done by the state or the courts themselves. In other words a fundamental part of the machinery of the common law, the reporting of cases of precedential value, is down to whether Bloggs or Snoops or Snodgrass is awake enough to be bothered to put pen to paper and can make a profit doing so.

Of course, it's going to be pretty obvious if a judgment is a biggy: it will have gone to the Supreme Court and all of the judges will have given their view of the law. And it will have been reported in All ER, WLR plus a few others and had learned articles written about it in MLR (Modern Law Review) and LQR (Law Quarterly Review) – the top periodicals in which leading law academics publish their expert views.

But the reason for this apparently haphazard reporting of decisions is historic. The development of English common law was intimately caught up with the way the king worked, although not all cases came before his court (lords and barons adjudicated on local disputes amongst their serfs). The king tended to be peripatetic, moving around amongst his subjects. This was partly to sponge off them, since his court numbered hundreds of civil servants and soldiers and they all needed feeding, and partly to impose his authority on his subjects by showing his face in a pre-media-and-celebrity age.

Over time parts of the king's operations were deposited at the palace of Westminster. The first was the Exchequer since money was weighty and the means of collecting it complex, requiring written records (in fact the name of the department comes from the chequered cloth covering the table on which the royal accounts were first recorded). This was soon followed by the curia regis (court of the king) around the time of Henry II and Richard I in the 12th century. It was under Henry II that judges started to sit regularly at Westminster as a central royal court or 'bench' while others continued to circulate with the king (hence the 'circuit judges' we still have today).

If you go to Westminster Hall you can imagine what it must have been like. It was built for William Rufus at the end of the 11th century and expanded by Richard II at the end of the 14th. This is where the key English courts sat until they moved to the Royal Courts of Justice in the Strand in 1882.

The Court of the King's Bench was divided by a flight of stairs from the Court of Chancery. The Exchequer was a separate room which connected to the main hall via a passage. On the west side was the Court of Common Pleas. Common pleas were those cases in which the king didn't have an interest and which therefore didn't come before the King's Bench (which is why the court was also known as Common Bench). The establishment of these two courts – King's Bench and Common Pleas – was a direct result of Magna Carta (clause 17), the showdown between the king and his subjects in 1215. The Court of Common Pleas is where the term 'common law' comes from.

Imagine the din and the stench. The judges in each court sat against the wall. The table before them (covered with a green cloth) would be used by the lawyers. There was nowhere for anyone except the judges to sit. The courts weren't screened off from one another nor from people crossing the hall. It must have seemed a 'bear pit' – the term that came to be used for the place in the Royal Courts of Justice where barristers congregate before and between court hearings.

You might think that the precedential value of cases – the spine of the common law system – followed inexorably from the fact that written records were kept of them. These records were called rolls because they were rolled up; the Exchequer's was called the 'great roll of the pipe', presumably because it was kept in a big tube; one of the top judges these days is still called the Master of the Rolls.

But in fact cases originally had no precedential value at all.

Eh?

The reason the first written records were kept was in order to teach budding lawyers-to-be how the courts worked and how decisions were arrived at, not to establish a database of precedents to which the courts themselves could refer.

You've got to laugh, really.

The power of the **common law system** came from the way it allowed subjects to raise issues (writs) and provide supporting arguments (pleadings) on which judges decided. Lawyers therefore needed to know how this system and the adjudicating courts worked. By the 1220s, lawyers were extracting interesting cases from the plea rolls and the first surviving records of judgments date from the 1250s.

These are not full transcripts but collections of dicta (statements) illustrating court procedures and pleadings or forms of action. These became accepted learning within the profession, set out as common learning (that word 'common' again) in the law books of the time. The first such legal treatise (written roughly around this time) was Bracton, named after the author. The judges were regarded as the principal exponents of common learning, not because their judgments carried precedential weight but because their judgments conformed to the established legal wisdom of the time.

The first law schools are where the **Inns of Court** are now (around Chancery Lane, Holborn and Gray's Inn Road) – in other words mid-town between the City (centre of commerce) and Westminster (centre of government, where the courts were). They taught writs, pleading and feudal land law. There are law schools there even now.

So cases were originally recorded to teach law students about the courts, not to establish precedents. And judgments weren't sources of law but merely evidence of what it was. This explains why the case reports that were kept didn't detail names of parties or claims but only the legal principles and the bare facts necessary to explain them. Of course, that has changed since, just as the role of the judges has. Expectations changed. As a principal source of law, cases were expected to provide increased certainty as to what the law was and where it would go.

English Legal History

You'd be forgiven for thinking that the law – or, at least, the volume of law we have these days – is unprecedented. But in fact medieval times were clogged up with law, especially highly complex laws relating to land.

By 1290 the old feudal system of land holding, begun by recording land rights in the Domesday Book, had broken down as lords found that tenants' duties were no longer being fulfilled. So Edward I passed a statute called Quia Emptores – every bit as important in its day as the Law of Property Act in 1925 – to clean up the law and ensure that the payment of taxes and the performance of duties passed with rights over land. If you're interested in this kind of stuff, then **English legal history** is an established discipline in its own right.

It's not without interest, not least since English common law is a study in legal archaeology anyway. For example, the modern magistrate is called a JP, short for **justice of the peace**. JPs have their origins in the king's practice begun in the 13th century of appointing local knights to 'keep the peace' and act as a modern-day police service. This included supplementing the role of local judges (called justices of assize) for instance in ensuring that criminals were carted off to gaol. The role of JPs was formalised under Edward III in 1361.

The tentacles of old law stretch into the present. For instance, the system of holding quarter sessions (hearings every three months to coincide with the seasons) which originated under Edward III was abolished only in 1971. Indeed, laws remain binding even if they fall into disuse. So, in 1818, the defendant in *Ashford v Thornton* caused consternation in court when he demanded trial by battle (a fight to the death or capitulation by sword), a way of settling cases that was introduced soon after 1066. This had been partly superseded by jury trials introduced as an alternative by Henry II in about 1180. But trial by battle was only finally revoked in 1963.

What I find fascinating about all of this is that we tend to think that law and its complexity is a modern invention. In fact, going back you realise that there was just as much law then as now – and that's ignoring a whole alternative system of law I haven't even touched on: **ecclesiastical law** as laid down by the church and enforced by ecclesiastical courts which over the centuries died out as the country became more secular. It was William I in fact who separated ecclesiastical and civil law, said to be the most significant legal change stemming from the Norman Conquest.

Which Bits Of Cases Establish Precedents

So that's how cases became valued as precedents. But in terms of precedential value, different bits of a case vary in importance. The **ratio decidendi** of a case is what it actually decided (Latin for the 'decided reason'). In other words, the important bit. The ratio is often called the 'held' by students because that's the bit in a case report, after the facts of the case have been given, in which the court reporter says what the court 'held' (decided).

It's often quite difficult to say what a court did hold. That's because hard cases get appealed up to the Court of Appeal (where there are three judges) and then the Supreme Court (where there are five). Each judge can give his or her own judgment. So the chances of them all saying the same thing is remote. Sometimes one judge will take the lead and the others will say simply that they agree ('I concur with my learned friend Lord Makepeace').

Where it gets hairy is where you have a **dissenting judgment** – in other words one or more judges disagree. If one out of three (in the CoA) or one or two out of five (in a Supreme Court case) dissent, it's called a **minority judgment** and you know you're in trouble because sooner or later another case will come along in which arguments are put in favour of the dissenting view.

But not everything a judge says may be relevant. Parts of his judgment may (in future cases that refer back to it) be declared 'obiter'. This is short for **obiter dictum** which means something said (dictum) around about (obiter): in other words, whatever was said wasn't directly on the legal point at issue so can be ignored. So subsequent judges can ignore what was said in a previous case by distinguishing their case (saying it's different) on the basis that the previous judge's view on the point was obiter ('obiter dicta' is the plural). So a later case may say a previous judge's pronouncements 'were obiter'.

Returning to the issue of whether judges actually make new law when interpreting the old, one solution is to pass a statute telling judges how to interpret statutes. New Zealand did. Its Interpretation Act told judges that every Act should be deemed remedial and so therefore receive the broadest interpretation to ensure its objective was achieved according to its true intent and spirit. The judges ignored it.

The other way is to turn the whole issue of whether judges make law into a philosophical discussion. This raises age-old questions concerning the law's relationship with morality and society. Let's take a look.

CHAPTER 11

JURISPRUDENCE: THE PHILOSOPHY OF LAW

Jurisprudence – philosophy of law – analytical – normative – natural law – reason – revelation – positivism – command theory – utilitarianism – rational empiricism – American realists – Hart-Fuller debate – economic analysis of law – sociological jurisprudence – socio-legal studies – critical legal studies

I've kept the best (or the worst) to last (depending on your point of view). This is **jurisprudence**, which is basically the **philosophy of law**. It's a whole area of legal study that's a bit like Dungeons & Dragons. You can get completely lost in it forever. Equally you may never venture in at all.

Jurisprudence is like your appendix: you can go your whole life as a lawyer without knowing it's there; and, even if you do, you're not quite sure if it's meant to do anything useful. Most practising lawyers don't give much of a toss about jurisprudence, so you can skip the rest of this chapter completely if you like (which is why I put it last). Confusingly, some law degrees are called 'degree in jurisprudence' but don't be taken in: they really are just law degrees.

Law And Philosophy

Jurisprudence is basically the philosophy of law. It's about how law is made, what it's for and why people obey it. It asks two types of question. First, what is the law and its role in, and relationship to, society? Second, what should the law be and to what extent does it reflect morality, however that is defined?

But over the last few decades jurisprudence has become a bit of a dustbin for any old '-ism' that has even a tangential connection with the law: anything from Marxism (did you know Karl Marx studied law, then philosophy – a sucker for punishment) to feminism and from structuralism and post-structuralism (schools of philosophy dealing with constructs implicit in language) to realism. Scandinavian realism, for example, rejects abstract inquiries into the nature of law and is only interested in propositions about law that can be empirically verified, that is, which can be actually observed.

The great (or not so great) thing about these questions is that there are no right or wrong answers, which means people can spend their lives debating these points.

So jurisprudence is the exploration of things legal outside the narrow technical question of what the law on any particular topic actually is. Some academics draw a distinction between the **analytical** (what is the law) and the **normative** (what makes for good law). As with all good academic debate there are different schools of thought and deeply-held views.

Law And Morality

Natural law says that any law that contravenes morality is wrong, and this standard is universal and is arrived at through **reason** (rational thought) or **revelation** (religion). Naturalists included the classical heavyweight triumvirate of Socrates, Plato and Aristotle. So you don't want to be messing with any of them.

But natural law is usually criticised for trying to get from 'is' to 'ought', that is, to move from fact or factual observation to a framework of morality, which however hard you try can't be done logically. If it could our lives would be so much easier, because there would be a single set of moral laws which would be above debate.

To be fair to Plato he did say that abiding by the law of the state was the highest moral obligation imposed on a citizen but there is a higher moral law against which state law is measured and may be found wanting.

Law And Society

Positivism rejects this attempt by natural law to link law to morality, saying instead that the only valid laws are those created by people in power in society. The law is an expression of human will, indeed of sovereign will (that of the top dog). So it favours an analytical approach in which correct decisions are logically arrived at. Positivists say there is no connection between law as it is and law as it should be, because moral judgments cannot be reached by rational argument.

This means that ultimately one must obey the law whatever it says (so divorcing it from morality and assuming that compliance results from the threat of sanction). The positivists tended to be people like Jeremy Bentham with his imperative view of the law (you obey it because you have to), known as the **command theory**, which has parallels with **utilitarianism** (you obey because that is what contributes to the greatest happiness of the most). As it happens, Bentham disliked lawyers and what he regarded as the legal system's 'exquisitely contrived chicanery'. Hegel too was a positivist and we all know where that led: to Nazi Germany (the absolute rule of law); since when jurisprudence has swayed back towards natural law.

However there is another school of thought, that of **rational empiricism**, which says that you need to look at the objective practice of the courts and what they really decide to answer these wider questions of the role of law in society and its relationship to morality. Realists reject metaphysical speculation on the nature of law. They don't like natural law much either. What they uphold is what you can verify empirically. The **American realists** go one further and say you have to look at what judges actually decide (not what they say they do or what the statute says) because before they have decided you don't know what they actually will decide.

The realist approach at least brings the debate down from a high level of philosophy and morality to the more practical level of how judges decide cases. Some positivists allow judges room to decide what are known as 'hard cases'. Ronald Dworkin, however, disagrees and says that, no matter how hard the case, there is always an objectively correct answer as to who should win. We'll come back to him in a moment.

A Third Way?

Herbert Hart regarded the positivists as too narrow and reintroduced the link between law and morality by focusing on language (law as an attempt to communicate the appropriate standards). So, for Hart, people obey the law because of sanctions (positivism) which are external and also because of a sense of duty (personal morality) which is internal.

Hart locked horns with Lon Fuller in what became known as the **Hart-Fuller debate**. Fuller believed in morality based on process, that is, legal systems which regulate human conduct through rules of law but which are themselves subject to rules which ensure moral standards are adhered to. Fuller reckoned there were eight such rules. Rules must:

- not be ad hoc pronouncements (otherwise erratic)
- not be retrospective (otherwise you don't know you're breaking one)
- be published (otherwise you don't know what they are)
- be intelligible (otherwise you don't know what they mean)
- not contradict each other (otherwise you don't know which to follow)
- be capable of compliance (otherwise what's the point)
- not be constantly changing (otherwise they're unpredictable)
- be in harmony with the rules and actions of those enforcing them (otherwise you're in trouble).

Fuller said that the more a system fulfils these rules the more 'moral' it is. Hart objected, saying that compliance with the eight rules doesn't necessarily lead to 'good' law.

Dworkin made himself unpopular all round, both with the positivists (he rejected Hart and the view that law and morality are distinct) and the naturalists (he rejected the idea of a higher or pre-determined morality against which law is judged).

For Dworkin, the problem with the positivists is that at heart (no pun intended) they see law as coming from a single, sovereign source (remember Bentham). So when there is no applicable law or it's contradictory (as in a hard case), a judge has discretion to decide. It comes down to language. Hart and the positivists have a narrow definition of what constitutes law. Dworkin extends the meaning of law to include policies and principles which all come together to make up society's moral fabric and to protect values upheld by society as a whole (such as the right to life, freedom and fairness).

Dworkin sees rules as being all or nothing. They cannot conflict with each other. But principles are different. They can conflict with each other. So therefore they need to be weighed up, measured, compared and so on. Judges have no discretion in the application of rules and even when weighing up principles there is a right answer, says Dworkin. If judges fail to reach it or fail to provide proper reasoning or explanation, this is because they are fallible humans, not because Dworkin is wrong. Dworkin imagined a superhuman, perfect judge called Hercules who isn't fallible and never gets the legal decision wrong. He could have been called Denning, perhaps.

Law As A Consumer Construct

Just returning to Bentham for a moment, there is a separate tributary (utilitarianism) that leads to another modern jurisprudential conception: **economic analysis of law** (EAL). Utilitarianism is about doing the best for the most. So utilitarians (who fall within the positivist camp) say that the purpose of law is to provide laws that maximise individual liberty.

Whereas Bentham saw utilitarianism in terms of pleasure and pain (a sort of hedonism based on the senses), John Stuart Mill was the thinking man's utilitarian, saying that the search for happiness was not simply sensual in origin, but could be intellectual; and was not hedonistic (focusing on the self) but altruistic (based on consideration of others).

For JSM, notions of justice were closely related to morality. He balanced personal freedom against possible harm to the interests of others. He also believed that the law should only intervene in areas of private moral conduct to the extent necessary to preserve public order and protect citizens, a modern view reflected over the last 50 years in the relaxation of laws on divorce, homosexuality, pornography and suicide.

The reason for returning to utilitarianism is that, if you substitute rational choice and the desire for economic efficiency in place of 'happiness', you are close to Richard Posner's school of EAL, a sort of utilitarianism for a consumer society where people are economic agents, maximising wealth and choice. Hence, people will obey the law rather than break it if the latter will make them worse off; and liability is a balance of economic consequence – if the measures to prevent a tort cost more than the damage caused by it, the courts will hold such measures to be an unreasonable imposition.

Rawls And Rights…

There's a lot more where this comes from. We haven't touched on individual rights (isn't having to stop at red lights an infringement of individual civil liberty? No, it's an administrative precaution to prevent pile-ups). Nor have we looked at justice as fairness. Above all we haven't encountered John Rawls who believed in an immutable set of values familiar to those brought up in western liberal democracies. Dworkin pops up here too. He, like Rawls, believes that protecting the rights of individuals is the bedrock of a just society.

This has morphed by way of **sociological jurisprudence** (law as a tool of social engineering, resolving competing claims) into **socio-legal studies** – a sort of social services version of jurisprudence where all of this philosophising about morality (which requires big brains and lots of time) is chucked out in favour of simply studying the legal system as it is, regardless of any theoretical underpinning, and seeing how it can be improved. Which when you've waded through all of this stuff seems either very appalling or very appealing indeed.

...Marx And Wrongs

But we're not done yet because talk of law and society takes us into the realms of Marxism which is pretty good in theory but rubbish in real life and **critical legal studies** (CLS) whose adherents aren't taken in by all of this philosophising either. They know it's just a smokescreen to hide the fact that law and its constructs are driven purely by the status quo of who is in power.

CLS emerged in the 1970s. Its earliest exponents were anti-Vietnam war activists from the 1960s who moved into academia the following decade. Inspired by Marx they attacked the apparent objectivity of the law in all its conservative institutionalism. Their successors have emerged in a variety of areas such as feminism and cultural studies which essentially look at law as a tool of social control by one group over others.

Law And Societal Values

My view for what it's worth is that law tends to reflect societal values (or to lag them somewhat) and to embody some natural principles of law (human rights) and, more or less, whatever the prevailing morality is. I know that last statement is a red rag to many people who believe that morality is and should be fixed and therefore absolute (what is right and wrong never changes). But, hey, life is too short and, besides, history is littered with things that no one would condone now but which were the norm at the time such as feudalism, spitting, smoking in public places and calling refuse operatives 'dustmen'.

So, to sum up, jurisprudence used to be about the philosophy of law and its relationship to morality; but is now much more about the role of law in society. Which means that you can take it or leave it. You don't need to know anything about jurisprudence to be interested in the law or to be a great lawyer. But if as a lawyer you want to know that what you're doing has a higher meaning, jurisprudence is where you may find it.

So that's it. We're done.

SUMMING UP:

A BASIC FRAMEWORK FOR UNDERSTANDING LAW

Hemingway started the final chapter of *Death In The Afternoon*, his magisterial account of matadors in Spain, with the words: 'If I could have made this enough of a book it would have had everything in it.'

The original version of this book was three times as long and tried to cram all of law in. That was patently impossible. The current edition of *Halsbury's Laws*, the famous legal encyclopedia, runs to 40-odd volumes. There are whole bookshops devoted to law (Hammicks in Fleet Street for one). So that was a foolish aim. Besides, the law is always changing. So it would have gone straight out of date.

But, most importantly, it's not what I wanted this book to be. It's meant to be a taster to give you an idea of what the law is like, not an authoritative survey of what the law actually is. There are loads of authoritative books out there about what the law is and I hope that this one will inspire you to go on to read some of them.

What Else To Read

The problem is that there are so many and they serve different purposes. So all I can begin to do here is navigate you through the field. Here are the different types:

Student textbooks This category forms the bulk of legal publishing, because there's an influx of new students each academic year and the law is always changing. The top legal publishers are Sweet & Maxwell (owned by Westlaw) and Butterworths (the imprint of LexisNexis). But there are other publishers in the field too including Oxford University Press (which owns legal publisher Blackstone, founded by the late great Alistair MacQueen) and the imprints of law schools such as CLP (the College of Law).

Textbooks fall into three groups: A-level and sixth form textbooks; law degree textbooks aimed at undergraduates doing traditional law courses at uni; and postgraduate textbooks for those doing the one-year GDL (graduate diploma in law) conversion course for non-law graduates and those doing the LPC (Legal Practice Course) or BPTC (Bar Professional Training Course) prior to becoming trainee solicitors or barristers.

Books in this category are mainly by subject (contract, tort, real estate, equity and trusts, etc) but there are introductory overviews for A-level students and overviews on topics such as the English Legal System.

Individual books or series that I like include:

- The *Nutshell* and *Nutcase* titles published by Sweet & Maxwell. Nutshells set out the law (there's one title per legal topic) and Nutcases provide synopses of the most relevant cases (again, one title per topic).

- The Routledge *Law Cards* series which are pocket-sized spiral-bound guides to a wide array of areas of law.

- The books by Elliott and Quinn (one's an academic, one's a legal journalist) published by Longmans that cover criminal, tort, contract and ELS.

- The materials produced by CILEx (the Chartered Institute of Legal Executives). But these may only be available for students undertaking CILEx courses to become legal executives.

A favourite student textbook of mine which I think is still published is *Riddell on Land Law* which I relied on at uni to learn real estate law.

Core textbooks These are used by students but also, crucially, by lawyers in practice (practitioners) to get a basic overview of a subject or to remind themselves of what they learnt at uni or law school. Well-known examples include Treitel (contract), Cheshire, Fifoot & Furmston (also contract), Megarry & Wade (real estate) and so on.

Practitioner texts These may look like core textbooks but they are in fact too complex, detailed or expensive for students. Instead they are used by practitioners as their core text in their field of practice and are often referred to in court. Law firms have them in their libraries. Examples include Benjamin (sale of goods), Bowstead & Reynolds (agency), Chitty (contracts), Clerk & Lindsell (torts), Gatley (libel and slander), Dicey (conflicts), Archbold (criminal), Kemp & Kemp (damages) and so on.

Encyclopedias These are multi-volume works that are found only in libraries of universities, law schools and law firms. Examples include *Halsbury's Laws*, the *Encyclopedia of Forms and Precedents* and *Atkin's Court Forms*.

So these are the types of law book that lawyers use to establish what the law is. But there are others too.

Practice management guides These are meant to help lawyers run their practices. They cover everything from how to keep accounts that comply with solicitors' regulations to how to look after clients, develop the business, establish a strategy and so on. Law firms have begun to attract heavy-weight management thinkers. Two whose books are worth seeking out are Stephen Mayson (*Making Sense of Law Firms*) and David Maister (*Managing the Professional Service Firm*).

Lawyer self-help guides These cover everything from how to become a lawyer to how to manage your career and so on. Examples include *Letters to a Law Student* by Nicholas McBride, *21st Century Solicitor* by Steve Weiner and *Why Lawyers Should Eat Bananas* (they're good for you) by Simon Tupman (however, I'm biased: I know the authors). If you're interested in being a barrister, Alex McBride has written *Defending the Guilty* which is his insight into what it's like to be a pupil (a trainee barrister).

Academic publications These form a completely different hinterland of legal publishing and are often the result of legal research submitted as a thesis to gain a PhD which is then published. Practitioners will sometimes consult these on abstruse points of law or to see where the law is heading. University funding depends in part on research activity which is why this sort of publishing is often encouraged amongst academics. Often they are comparative law studies, comparing similar laws under different legal systems.

Law-in-society books You are much more likely to read these than academic publications. These books occasionally become bestsellers and are written by legal journalists and broadcasters, social and political commentators or campaigning writers. They examine the changing role of law in society or uncover injustice.

Assistance with legal issues for lay readers These books are designed to help people who aren't lawyers tackle legal issues they encounter in their lives without, or before they use, a lawyer. The principal areas covered are: making wills; enduring powers of attorney (for use with elderly relatives); getting a divorce; buying and selling a house. Your best bet is to look online, in a library or in any large bookstore. The Consumers' Association which publishes *Which?* magazine publishes legal self-help guides. It's also worth looking on government websites for advice.

Books about lawyers Finally there are books about lawyers (such as Denning and, more recently, the famous barrister George Carman) and where they work (for instance tracing the history of the Inns of Court in London). These are usually only of interest to other lawyers and fellow professionals.

Online materials You may be interested to know that the large law firms are big buyers of legal materials. The bulk of these are provided online and there is a complete industry of online legal and business information providers to law firms, with their own conferences and trade exhibitions.

So that's what else you can read. Finally, I need to return to where we started. I said at the outset that I had expected the law to be well-ordered – a well laid-out city, a Palladian temple – and instead I found it to be a shanty town. I don't know about you but I can only grasp things if I have a simple structure or framework to put them in. Having taken you on a whistle-stop tour of the law and the legal profession I thought you might find it helpful to try to squeeze it all into some order. Here goes.

A Basic Framework For Understanding Law

One way of looking at the law is to set it out (and the contents of this book) under five headings:

1.   **What The Law Is** (covered in Chapters 1, 2, 4, 5, 6) comprising the five core subjects: criminal, tort, contract, property and equity (I put equity before property when I explained them earlier so you could understand property which is so dependent on the concept of trusts and equitable rights. But in

my own mind the first four are 'legal' law and the fifth is 'equitable' law so I put them here in that order). These are the underpinnings of law. I call them the pillars of law.

2. **How Law Develops** (Chapters 3, 7, 8 and the Appendix) which includes all the modern branches and specialisations of law, such as private client, wills and probate, charities, matrimonial, corporate, shipping, banking, employment, pensions, intellectual property, tax, EU and competition, human rights, public law, social and housing law and so on. This is, if you like, law in practice.

3. **How Law Is Made** (Chapters 3, 8, 10, 11) which explains how the areas of law in 2 are added to and expand. So this is about the role of Parliament (how the legislature makes law). It's also about the common law (the precedential value of cases) and so therefore English legal history. It's about the role of law in society, the relationship between law and morality and the philosophy of law, all of which is jurisprudence. It's about comparing legal systems (comparative law) which is one example of the role of the academic in law whose job is to elucidate, identify gaps (lacunae) and look forward to future developments (as well as teach, obviously).

4. **How Law Is Applied** (Chapters 3, 10) is the very practical day-to-day workings of the law. So this is about the courts, their procedures, the costs, awards and sanctions. It's about the English Legal System, the difference between the criminal and civil courts, their rules of evidence and the differing burdens of proof and the hierarchy of courts (how cases get appealed up the system, called the appellate system). It's about what you get when you go to court (court orders such as injunctions and damages) or are convicted of a crime (a sentence) and whether prison really works (recidivism). It's about the costs of going to court, legal aid and funding, and periodic reviews of the court system and procedures (the Woolf reforms being the most notable in recent history).

5. **What Lawyers Do** (Chapters 3, 7, 9) is about types of lawyer, what they do and how they work and organise themselves. So under this heading comes discussion of barristers and solicitors, chambers and partnerships, in-house lawyers who work in the legal departments of companies (private sector) or public bodies (public sector), as well as other types of lawyer such as legal executives, paralegals, licensed conveyancers and (now rather rare) notaries and scriveners. It's about criminal and civil lawyers, contentious and non-contentious, private client and legal aid lawyers, high street solicitors and commercial firms that serve business clients, as well as national and international law firms. It's also about how to become a lawyer.

Periodic Table

I said at the beginning that the Periodic Table was a nightmare when I was a student. It isn't any more. It's sleek and well-ordered (although it has grown over time, from 63 elements when Dmitri Mendeleev created it in 1869 to almost double that now). So I've developed my own version for law, which is a slight variation on what I've just covered above. You've already seen it. It's just before the Introduction at the start of the book.

A Final Word Of Warning

This isn't really a law book. That's to say it isn't meant to be an accurate statement of the law at a particular date and so will not be revised year-on-year. This means you could be reading these words years after I wrote them (the way we see light from stars long dead). So cases I mention may have been overruled and legislation repealed. So go and read some real law books now. And I haven't just put this caveat in because it's what lawyers do.

APPENDIX:
AREAS OF LEGAL PRACTICE

This is a list of the practice areas I've been referring to throughout. I thought you might find it helpful to have a list of them in one place in alphabetical order (but it is very boring so don't try to read it all the way through). Note, however, that law is always developing and spawning new specialisations, so this list may be out of date even as you read it.

Many of these specialisations are based on contract. But as they develop they become very different from each other, especially in their terminology which comes to reflect the industry they underpin (such as banking, insurance, shipping, media and so on).

It's why you can meet a lawyer who specialises in, say, employment law, and he or she will profess to know nothing about buying or selling a house. They may have done once upon a time as a student or when they were training to be a lawyer but now they are qualified and specialist they only ever deal with employment matters so that's all they know about in detail.

Here's the list.

Administrative law is a slightly odd one to kick off the list since it is not that visible publicly. It's about the interface between government and the governed. It hits the headlines whenever a government minister is taken to court because a decision of his or her department is being questioned. This is called judicial review. There are other equally obscure procedures. One is called mandamus ('show us') which is about whether government has actually done what it's supposed to. This is more an academic branch of law than one practised widely in law firms. See also constitutional.

Admiralty is an aspect of shipping and divides into 'wet' and 'dry'. Wet is basically about ships hitting things (like jetties) and each other. It includes the law of salvage – the rights of those who save a ship to keep it or at least receive some reward. Since radar is improving all the time ships hit each other and sink less often than they used to. Dry admiralty is about cargoes (for more on this see shipping). A small number of substantial London law firms specialise almost exclusively in shipping, international trade and commodities law.

Art law is relatively new. It's about the rights of artists to participate in the proceeds of sale of their works as these pass from hand to hand. The art world is an industry in its own right with dealers, agents, galleries and auction houses. The law of auction is becoming a specialist area in its own right – there have been laws applicable to markets for centuries. Again, all of this is based on contract. Art law is in some respects a branch of media.

Banking, Asset Finance And Project Finance (aka **Debt Finance**) is a huge area of law (especially internationally where English and New York law are the dominant systems) and forms the core practice of many of the world's largest law firms. Again it is based on contract but much specialist law has developed around the taking of security (the lender taking a charge over the borrower's assets in order to be able to sell them if the borrower fails to repay the loan). It includes the law on guarantees and sureties. This is where banking law shades into insolvency. Asset finance (aka finance leasing or equipment leasing) is a way of financing big things like planes and ships where the bank owns the asset and leases it to the business that wants to use it. Project financing is about funding infrastructure developments, such as power stations, dams, roads, harbours and airports, train stations, hospitals and schools. It allows for the fact that these projects can take years to complete before there is any payback. It overlaps with construction and engineering. Banking law (which includes all of these) is also known as debt finance to distinguish it from equity finance because it is based on making loans and getting repaid.

Business law is an umbrella term for a number of specialisations including company, commercial and employment. It also includes forms of doing business aside from being incorporated (being a company) such as being a sole trader or in partnership with others. It includes buying and selling businesses, usually private companies (whereas M&A is generally about the takeover of large, public companies). It also extends to forms of financing SMEs (small and medium sized enterprises) including some aspects of debt finance (such as loans) and equity finance (such as venture capital). Lawyers in smaller firms may act for SMEs, such as newsagents and estate agents; those in larger firms act for substantial businesses.

Capital Markets is the international version of debt finance and equity finance. It means the raising of money by issuing bonds (debt) or shares (equity) usually involving an investment bank to arrange the issue. These bonds or shares are known collectively as securities (not to be confused with the taking of security where 'security' means a 'charge') and are issued internationally and not just in the UK. London is a leading international financial centre. English and New York law are the two dominant systems of law under which these types of financing are written. The biggest and most international law firms dominate this field.

Charities law is about the law governing charitable institutions. The charitable or not-for-profit sector (the 'third sector' as it is known, to distinguish it from the public and private sectors) is huge in the UK. But, quite apart from well-known charities such as the RSPCA and Cancer Research, many organisations are charities in legal structure, including most private schools. Local authorities often need advice on charities law because of land left to them in the past for charitable purposes.

Child law is now a specialisation in its own right. It's to do with the welfare and rights of children and (in my view) has emerged from two areas of law: matrimonial, which determines what happens to couples and their children when the couple divorce; and welfare law which is about the duties of the state (local and central government) to disadvantaged people. So child law will typically extend to orphans, children in care and the basis on which they are taken into care, as well as adoption (since many more couples these days wish to adopt and some appeal against decisions turning their applications down).

Commercial law covers agency, distribution and joint ventures and is the law of business. Businesses need all sorts of law, such as company (if they operate as companies), employment (staff), commercial property (premises), banking (loans) and so on. Commercial is about the contracts that businesses enter into. The reason why agency and distribution are singled out is because a lot of commercial contracts are about manufacturers getting others to distribute their products. If an agent does it, they sell goods on your behalf and you pay them a commission. If a distributor, they effectively buy the goods off you and keep whatever they make from the on-sale. Supply agreements (where a supplier supplies something – say a farmer supplying produce to a supermarket) are also commercial agreements. A joint venture is when two commercial parties come together to run a business venture together. All of these are based on the law of contract but agency is an established sub-branch of contract in its own right.

Commercial Property is a subset of real estate which we covered in Chapter 6. Most major buildings and developments (such as shopping centres) are owned by big institutional investors such as insurance companies and pension funds, as well as property companies and property developers. Commercial property is about the development and management of these buildings. It includes, at one end, site acquisition and, at the other, the letting of offices, warehouses and shops. Related areas of law include planning, construction and debt finance (when debt is used to fund real estate it is called 'property finance'). Once commercial property has been let the applicable specialisation is called 'landlord & tenant' where the landlord is the institutional investor and the tenant is the business that occupies the premises. It covers topics such as the right of the tenant to assign (sell) the lease and the repairs ('dilapidations') it has to put right. Since institutional investors often own hundreds and indeed thousands of these properties, landlord & tenant at this level is often called 'property management'.

Commodities are goods that are transported round the world, ranging from hard commodities like steel to soft foodstuffs like coffee, tea and cocoa. Most commodities are traded on commodity exchanges or simply between parties in what is called the spot market. Commodities law applies to such transactions but extends to the transport and insurance of commodities (see shipping and international trade). Such deals are often financed through trade finance which is an aspect of banking law.

Company law is the law relating to the establishment and running of companies including the rights of shareholders and the duties of directors. Every so often the government revises company law. Recent revisions have included the Companies Acts of 1948, 1967, 1985 and, most recently, 2006.

Competition law (aka **European Union** or **EU** law) concerns legislation laid down by the EU to prevent businesses gaining a monopoly. This is part of the underlying purpose of the EU, to create a single market place where businesses can compete against each other across national boundaries. Competition law is particularly relevant to M&A (mergers and acquisitions). When one big public company takes over another it has to be careful that the resulting business will not be 'market dominant' which is against EU law. Competition law is only one aspect of EU law. But it's the one that affects business the most, which is why EU has come to be shorthand amongst corporate lawyers for competition law.

Conflicts Of Laws See private international law.

Constitutional law (usually bracketed with administrative law as 'admin and consti') is the law about government, how law is made, the rights of the individual in relation to the state and so on. The UK doesn't have a written constitution so citizens' rights are enshrined in common law, that is, case law over the ages. Magna Carta (1215) could be said to be the first piece of constitutional law in the modern era.

Construction And Engineering law (usually bracketed together) is just another form of contract law, involving big building projects. This is a highly specialised area in its own right for two reasons: first, the terminology and jargon of the construction industry require specialist knowledge; second, almost all construction contracts lead to some form of dispute. It's part and parcel of the industry. Most project financings (debt finance) involve construction contracts.

Consumer law is the umbrella term for legislation that protects consumer rights, such as the Sale of Goods Act 1979 (SOGA) and the Unfair Contract Terms Act 1977 (UCTA). Both vary the underlying contract between retailer and consumer. In particular, SOGA says that goods have to be of satisfactory quality. UCTA specifies when a retailer or manufacturer cannot exclude liability for damage caused by defective goods. See also product liability.

Corporate is used to describe what City lawyers (and bankers) do in relation to companies: helping them list on the London Stock Exchange (when they move from being private companies to public companies because their shares are now publicly traded and anyone can buy them); and helping them take each other over (M&A – mergers and acquisitions). The actual law involved is a combination of company law (under the Companies Acts), financial services law, Stock Exchange regulations and Takeover Panel rules (the Takeover Panel is the body that polices public takeovers) as set out in the Takeover Code.

Criminal law is the body of law covered in Chapter 1: the law imposed by the state on the citizen to enable society to function, by preserving life, limb and property.

Defamation is an area of tort law that prevents individuals' reputations from being impugned by others. Libel is what is written; slander is what is said.

Education is a relatively new area of law and, like all new areas of law, is a ragbag that brings together some strands of established law that otherwise exist in isolation from each other. So some of it is charity law (which is what most schools and colleges are); some is regulatory (a succession of Education Acts: government laws in relation to education); some is about the rights of the individual to be educated; some is trade union law in relation to teachers; some is the law relating to premises and health & safety; some is the law relating to children and social services.

Employment law is the body of complex rules and cases that apply to employment, employees and employers. Much of this law is about the reasons for which employees can be sacked or made redundant; some is about maternity rights, including flexible working. It all tends to be complex, revolving around time limits and notice periods. Lawyers specialising in the field tend to fall into those who do contractual work and those who take cases to employment tribunals; they also tend to divide into those who act for employees (smaller firms) and those acting for employers (larger firms) plus a handful specialising in acting for trade unions and employees whose unions provide legal advice and representation for them. The rights of employees extend to their rights on retirement – see pensions.

Energy, Oil And Gas law is an example of the sector-specific areas of law that have developed over the past few decades (shipping and banking being amongst the earliest). This area of law divides into two: upstream and downstream activities. **Upstream** is about getting the oil and gas out of the ground or, in the case of electricity, generating it. It can cross over with project finance and includes mining rights and other contractual relations between governments, landowners and businesses involved in extracting, generating and transport. Oil pipelines that run for hundreds of miles across inhospitable territory require construction agreements, licences and distribution agreements. **Downstream** activity is about marketing, selling, distributing and transporting energy, as well as health & safety and other regulatory aspects. This sort of work tends to be the preserve of the larger law firms because it draws upon so many specialisations.

Environment is closely related to planning and commercial property from which it first emerged as an area of law principally affecting land and the uses to which it is put. Originally, the first environmental lawyers tended to sit within planning and property departments of firms. That's now changed. Environmental law is a specialisation in its own right and the latest sub-specialisation is trading in carbon credits which is closely related to commodities. Environmental law is as likely to involve international carbon trading as it is industrial pollutants of rivers, for example. As global climate change leads to extreme weather and flooding so environmental law overlaps with regulatory law as well as litigation against builders, planning authorities, local and central government. Lawyers acting for related businesses (such as waste disposal and landfill) will often be lawyers specialising in commercial law.

Equity See wills, trusts & probate.

Equity Finance (not to be confused with equity) is the money that shareholders put into businesses so equity finance is about companies issuing shares (usually public companies doing so on the London Stock Exchange) and taking each other over (M&A) by offering their shares for the target's. Equity finance also overlaps with private equity since it includes acting for providers of equity finance such as private equity funds, hedge funds and institutional investors (pension funds and insurance companies). The issuing of shares internationally is called 'equity capital markets' (see capital markets).

Family law is another name for matrimonial (divorce) and child law.

Financial Services (including **Funds**) is the complex set of laws, rules and regulations that apply to financial markets and the protection of those who invest in them. One aspect of it is called 'funds' and this is the creation, regulation and marketing of investment funds such as unit trusts to the public. Any attempt to raise money by way of public issues (such as promoting shares to the public for them to buy) is heavily regulated to avoid fraud. Much of it concerns the detail of what an investment manager or promoter of a fund or issue can and can't say when marketing that issue. It is closely related to equity finance and corporate work since companies issue shares when they list on the London Stock Exchange and to finance takeovers (M&A) of other companies.

Franchising is a business format, that is, a way of carrying on business. It's most closely associated with fast-food retail chains and is a way of establishing a brand quickly and with the least amount of capital. Instead of owning all the outlets (which takes time and money) a franchisor devises a brand and then licenses it to individuals or small businesses (franchisees), each of whom runs one or more outlets. The franchisor provides support (materials bearing the brand and logo, training, etc) and the franchisees will pay a percentage of their taking as a royalty or licence fee. The public gets the comfort of a uniform brand and service offering, the franchisor receives income from licence fees and the franchisees obtain much greater brand awareness, market penetration and support than if each were on his or her own. The law is mainly around commercial agreements. It is therefore a subset of commercial and business law.

Fraud And Asset Tracing is a form of litigation or dispute resolution, that is, contentious rather than non-contentious work. In other words it involves cases before the courts. Some of these may be criminal – acting for someone accused of fraud; some may be civil – seeking the return of assets that have been stolen. Often a financial institution will obtain a freezing order that stops someone dealing with a bank account or other financial assets. These days culprits will move assets in and out of bank accounts and financial centres so cases are often international. Actions will be brought in a variety of countries to try to stop the fraudsters in their tracks and recover whatever has been pilfered or purloined.

Housing law is about the rights of individual tenants (known as residential tenants), many of whom are housed by their local authority (which is their landlord) or depend on welfare benefits to pay the rent. See also welfare.

Immigration law is a developed specialisation within social and welfare law and means acting for individuals seeking to stay in the UK. At an executive level it is an aspect of employment law (acting for multinational companies moving senior people around the world) but the bulk of cases involve people of limited or no means coming from developing economies and seeking to stay for economic benefit (to work) or political reasons (seeking asylum and safety from persecution in their country of origin). Lawyers who do this work are almost always fighting cases against the Home Office.

Insolvency is the law that applies when a business goes bust. When its outgoings exceed its income and it can no longer pay creditors, it is said to be insolvent (in the case of an individual this is called bankruptcy). It's a technically demanding area of law that lays down who gets what, in which order, when a business ceases. The challenge is that there are usually fewer assets than there are claims, and lenders tend to have competing interests. A bank will have a charge over a borrower's assets so that if the borrower defaults on the loan the bank can seize the assets and sell them to recompense its loss (this is where insolvency and debt finance meet). But lenders are not the only creditors. Others may include employees, suppliers, customers and HM Revenue & Customs. In addition the directors of the business may have favoured some creditors over others in the run-up to the insolvency. This is called a preference and can be set aside. Suppliers may themselves reserve title to their goods pending payment and may 'trace' their claim directly to those goods if they still exist. This retention of title is called a *Romalpa* clause after the case that first upheld it.

Insurance And Reinsurance law is closely linked to shipping. It isn't so much about the primary insurance market (where individuals and businesses take out insurance cover) but about the contracts that insurers take out with reinsurers to offload some of the risk they have underwritten. Reinsurance is an international business, much of it carried on in London (Lloyd's of London is the world's biggest reinsurance market) so contracts and claims tend to be international. Much of the work is litigious (that is, about taking cases to court) because large claims are almost always resisted. It's an area of law that has its own language ('cedants', 'retrocessionaires', 'treaties', 'facultative') and is closely linked to shipping because the maritime world is one of the biggest users of insurance (for ships and cargoes).

Intellectual Property is the broad term for the law covering copyright, trademarks and patents. Patent work is also done by specialist patent attorneys (basically scientists with legal qualifications) and is the most technical end of IP law since it involves the protection of technical innovations. Trademark law is about the protection and commercial exploitation of brands and logos which in these image-conscious days can be worth hundreds of millions of dollars (think of Coke and the Nike swoosh). Copyright is the legal protection that automatically arises when someone creates something literary, musical or artistic (see the copyright notice at the front of this book). All three are labelled IP because they are about the ownership (property) of the fruits of mental (intellectual) creativity.

International Trade overlaps with shipping since it involves contracts for the cross-border supply of goods and commodities, usually involving transport and insurance considerations.

Landlord & Tenant is a sub-specialisation of commercial property. Almost all businesses, from high street newsagents to multinational companies, rent their premises from institutional investors like insurance companies and pension funds that own the freeholds of most commercial properties in the UK. There's a lot of law around the protection of tenants, whether business tenants or individuals. L&T is about acting for business tenants or their landlords. Individual (residential) tenants who get into disputes with their landlords tend to be poor so residential L&T is known as housing law and is part of welfare law.

Matrimonial is part of family law and is about divorce, the rights of and duties towards children on divorce (including custody and access – see child law) and, crucially, the financial arrangements between the divorcing parties (including pensions). It extends to advice prior to marriage (such as pre-nuptial contracts) as well as on alternatives to marriage (such as co-habitation and civil partnerships).

M&A (mergers & acquisitions) is the law governing takeovers of and by public companies (that is, companies listed on the London Stock Exchange). It's related to company law.

Media law is a relatively recent specialisation and is an umbrella term for a number of different strands. It includes publishing (hard copy and electronic) of books, magazines and newspapers; broadcasting (television, radio); multimedia (including video games and DVD); and the exploitation of the associated commercial rights. A lawyer who acts for actors or authors can be said to practise media law, as can someone who acts for an F1 racing team or football team or someone representing a TV production company or broadcasting channel. See also music and sports law. The exploitation of commercial rights is an extension of intellectual property (brands, trademarks and licensing).

Medical Negligence is a specialist area of tort law and is about suing healthcare providers for failing to meet adequate standards of service provision, for instance if a surgical procedure goes wrong. The most harrowing cases involve children severely damaged at birth. Much of the law is about assessing liability (whether anyone is liable) and quantum (the level of damages to be awarded). In the case of children the damages can run to millions of pounds to provide for their care for the rest of their lives.

Music was one of the founding areas of what is now called media law. At heart it involves acting for artistes, promoters, publishers, venues and record companies. As the music industry has been disintermediated by the internet (downloading replacing CD sales) so the traditional source of artistes' income (royalties) has now been superseded by broader rights exploitation, live events and broadcasting.

Neighbour Disputes are not a separate area of law but a combination of residential property law and tort (nuisance or *Rylands v Fletcher* – see Chapter 6).

Pensions law concerns the rights and obligations arising out of pension funds. At its heart it is about trust law since pension funds are constituted by trust deeds. But it is much broader than that. The idea that employers (companies) should provide pensions to their employees to support them in retirement came from the Quaker movement (Cadbury's, the chocolate confectioner, was one such). A pension fund is separate from the company (called the sponsor) whose employees belong to it. It is run by trustees for the benefit of members (current and future pensioners). The trustees have duties to members, for instance in relation to the investment of pension fund assets (which comprise contributions made by employer and employees) out of which pensions are paid. Pensions law used to be considered a backwater but now many M&A deals hinge on the level of the target company's pension fund liabilities. See also employment.

Personal Injury is an aspect of tort law and involves making claims on behalf of individuals, usually following industrial accidents or tripping over pavements. It can overlap with insurance law since those sued tend to be companies or local authorities that are insured to cover such claims.

Planning (called 'zoning' in the US) is about what you can build where. It is usually practised by lawyers who started out in commercial property and specialised further. Some major developments are subject to public inquiries that can go on for years (for instance, an airport wishing to add or extend a runway).

Private International Law (aka conflicts of laws) is about which system of law governs an international contract and which courts can hear the case on it. It also leads to something called 'forum shopping' – trying to find a country whose courts will favour your argument the most. English law on libel has for years been regarded as overly generous to claimants bringing cases against newspapers, paparazzi and publishers and has attracted cases between parties who otherwise have little connection (and whose case has little connection) with the UK.

Probate See wills, trusts & probate.

Product Liability is an aspect of tort and involves representing companies accused of it (big manufacturers such as car makers, for instance) or consumers who have suffered as a result, often involving 'class actions' (imported from the US) where one law firm will act for hundreds of individuals in one big court case against the manufacturer rather than each of them having to bring a separate claim on his or her own. See also consumer law which is about the extent to which liability for faulty products can be excluded by the terms written into the consumer contract (not much is the answer, and not at all where death results).

Professional Indemnity is another aspect of tort, involving advice given negligently by professionals such as accountants, surveyors and, er, solicitors. There are lawyers and law firms that specialise in defending professionals against such claims. It is related to insurance since most professionals and professional service firms are insured against negligence.

Public International Law is the law between countries and is used to settle boundary disputes, fishing rights and rights to coastal waters. It also underpins weightier matters such as the law of war and when legal title is acquired by a victorious occupying force.

Residential Property or **Conveyancing** involves the same law as commercial property but is really about the mechanics of buying and selling flats and houses (see Chapter 6). It is about automating the process to make it as cheap for consumers as possible.

Securities law is an aspect of capital markets which is about the issue and trading of shares (equity) and bonds (debt). The two are known collectively as 'securities' (not to be confused with 'taking security' which is the legal term for taking a mortgage over property or a charge over other assets as security for a loan). Because there is a lot of law around the issue of securities and the extent to which they can be sold to the public (to prevent fraud), this aspect of capital markets is about the regulations affecting the issue of shares or bonds.

Shipping traditionally involves 'wet admiralty' (the law about collisions between ships) and 'dry admiralty' (the law surrounding the transport of cargo). Both have their own terminology. So 'salvage' concerns the rights of those who rescue cargo (and the wreck itself) when a ship sinks. 'Freight' is the charge for carrying goods. A 'bill of lading' is evidence of the contract of carriage, is receipt for the goods, and evidence of title to the goods – this last means the goods can be sold on while still at sea. The Italians invented the bill of lading and its forerunner was in use in the ancient city of Carchemish in the 7th century BC. Since shipping is almost by definition international, it is also necessarily about international trade which is why it overlaps with commodities law (commodities can be hard or soft – hard ones like steel, soft ones like coffee and cocoa – they are the cargo you put on board ships). Because contracts are international and cross jurisdictional boundaries, some of the issues fall within conflicts of laws. Also related to insurance and reinsurance.

Sports law originally involved the rights of athletes and sportsmen in relation to their employers (such as football clubs). Now it extends to the commercial exploitation of brands and so is part of media law.

Tax is about advising individuals and companies on the impact of taxation. Every transaction of a business or bank generally involves tax considerations. It is complex – and because the government is forever dreaming up new ways of taxing its citizenry (whether individual or corporate) or amending what is already there, it's an area of law that is always changing and involves something most lawyers hate: numbers.

Technology law started off as the law relating to computing – essentially a form of commercial law involving the buying and selling of technology. But it soon developed into the law relating to data – for instance, when is an electronic signature valid – and now includes data protection legislation. A lot of big outsourcing deals (where a business gets someone else to run part of its operations) are essentially about outsourcing a business's technology requirements to a specialist provider so although outsourcing includes more general, commercial transactions that don't have to involve technology at all, a lot of technology lawyers have moved into that area. Technology also necessarily overlaps with intellectual property which is about ownership of the content (whereas technology is about platforms). As platforms have converged, so technology, television, media and telecoms have converged too. Now with platforms (TV, DVDs, devices, downloads, streaming) and content (films, music, video games, news) converging, technology, media and intellectual property are often combined practices in the largest firms.

Telecoms is the law surrounding telecommunications. It wasn't an area of practice prior to the privatisation of British Telecom in 1984. That created a new industry with a whole regulatory infrastructure in which lawyers started to specialise.

Trade Union law is often undertaken by law firms that specialise in employment law but it's much more about the organisation of employee representative bodies and their rights in relation to and on behalf of their members (employees) against employers. It's because a large part of the protection that trade unions provide to their members is about employment rights (and, for instance, compensation for injury at work) that lawyers doing this work also do employment, personal injury and health & safety work.

Welfare law is the term applied to the bundle of rights that those on social welfare have, ranging from free or subsidised housing and debt advice to claiming asylum or community care. Much of it is provided by law centres or the Citizens Advice

Bureau, both of which seek to widen access to the legal system. See also housing law.

Wills, Trusts & Probate is well known to you from Chapter 5. Wills are the documents people draw up dealing with their estates when they die (saying who will get what). Trusts are legal structures that separate legal ownership from beneficial enjoyment of the financial return from ownership, often used by people when drawing up their wills to leave property to a succession of people or to children. Probate is the legal business of administering an estate and distributing it to the beneficiaries of the will. Trusts is part of equity law which grew up alongside the common law to give equitable redress where application of the strict law itself would have led to a harsh outcome.

The following index also serves as a glossary. Turn to the page where a term is first mentioned and that should be where its meaning is given.

INDEX / GLOSSARY